SUCH A LOVELY
LITTLE WAR

MARCELINO TRUONG

SUCH A LOVELY LITTLE WAR

SAIGON 1961-63

TRANSLATED BY DAVID HOMEL

ARSENAL
PULP PRESS

SUCH A LOVELY LITTLE WAR: Saigon 1961-63
by Marcelino Truong
English-language translation © 2016 by David Homel

SECOND PRINTING: 2018

First published in French as *Une si jolie petite guerre: Saigon 1961-63*
© 2012 Editions Denoël

ARSENAL PULP PRESS
Suite 202 – 211 East Georgia St.
Vancouver, BC V6A 1Z6
Canada
arsenalpulp.com

This book has received support from the Institut français' Publication Support Programmes.

This book has been supported by the French Ministry of Foreign Affairs as part of the translation grant program.
Cet ouvrage est soutenu au titre des programmes d'aide à la publication du Ministère des Affaires étrangères.

The publisher also gratefully acknowledges the support of the Government of Canada (through the Canada Book Fund) and the Government of British Columbia (through the Book Publishing Tax Credit Program) for its publishing activities.

Canada

Editing of translation by Brian Lam
Design of translated edition by Oliver McPartlin
Original design by Marion Tigréat/Les Associés Réunis
Printed and bound in Korea

Library and Archives Canada Cataloguing in Publication:
 Truong, Marcelino
[Si jolie petite guerre. English]
    Such a lovely little war : Saigon, 1961-63 / Marcelino
Truong.

Translation of: Une si jolie petite guerre.
Issued in print and electronic formats.
ISBN 978-1-55152-647-8 (paperback).—ISBN 978-1-55152-648-5
(html).—ISBN 978-1-55152-649-2 (epub)

    1. Truong, Marcelino—Comic books, strips, etc. 2. Vietnam
War, 1961-1975—Personal narratives, Vietnamese—Comic books,
strips, etc. 3. Graphic novels. I. Title. II. Title: Si jolie petite
guerre. English

DS556.93.T77A313 2016   959.704'3092   C2016-903231-0
                                              C2016-903232-9

"Perhaps it's true that people are simply the product of their times."
—Alexis Jenni, *L'art français de la guerre (The French Art of War)*, 2011

"Independence, yes, but not just any kind. We must learn to distrust noble causes. In general, they are like the con artist's suitcase, full of hidden compartments."
—Serge July, *Libération*, April 30, 1985

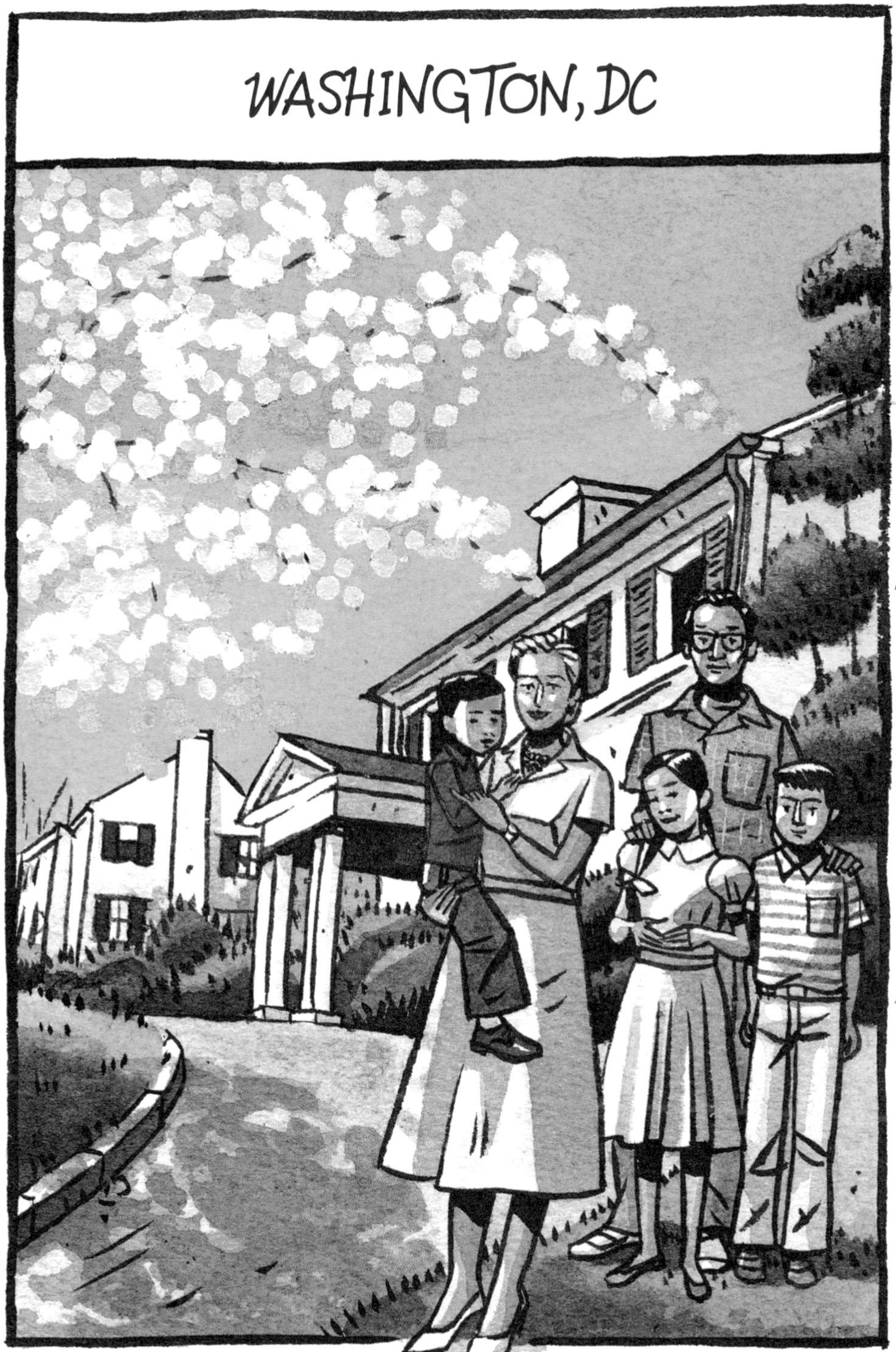
WASHINGTON, DC

May 1961. Washington, DC. The White House ---

The Lincoln Memorial ---

Arlington National Cemetery ---

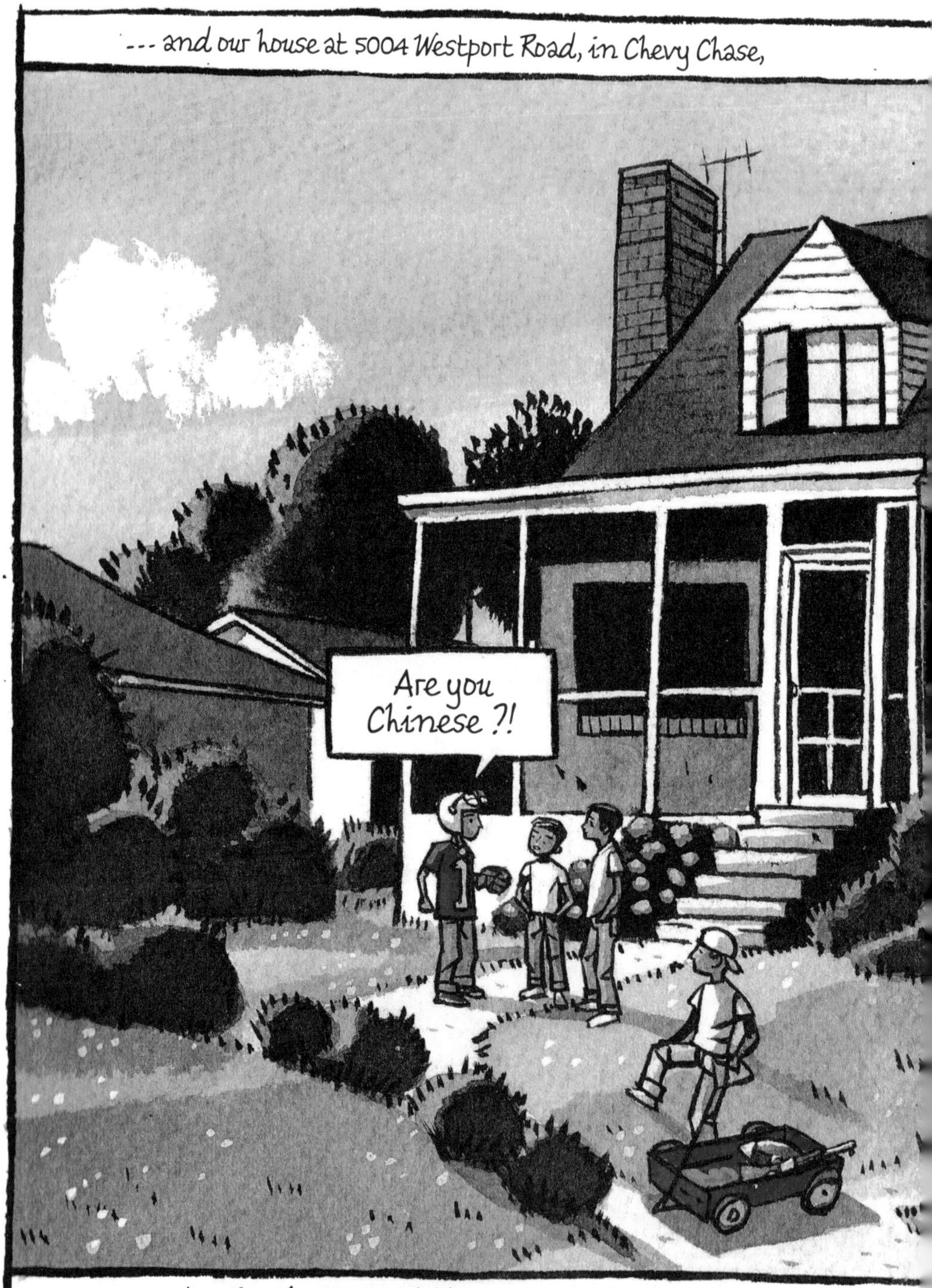
--- and our house at 5004 Westport Road, in Chevy Chase,
Are you Chinese ?!
America the Beautiful, like a Peanuts cartoon.

a quiet middle-class suburb, something Norman Rockwell might imagine.

Complete with cherry pie, a corner store, and Coca-Cola ---

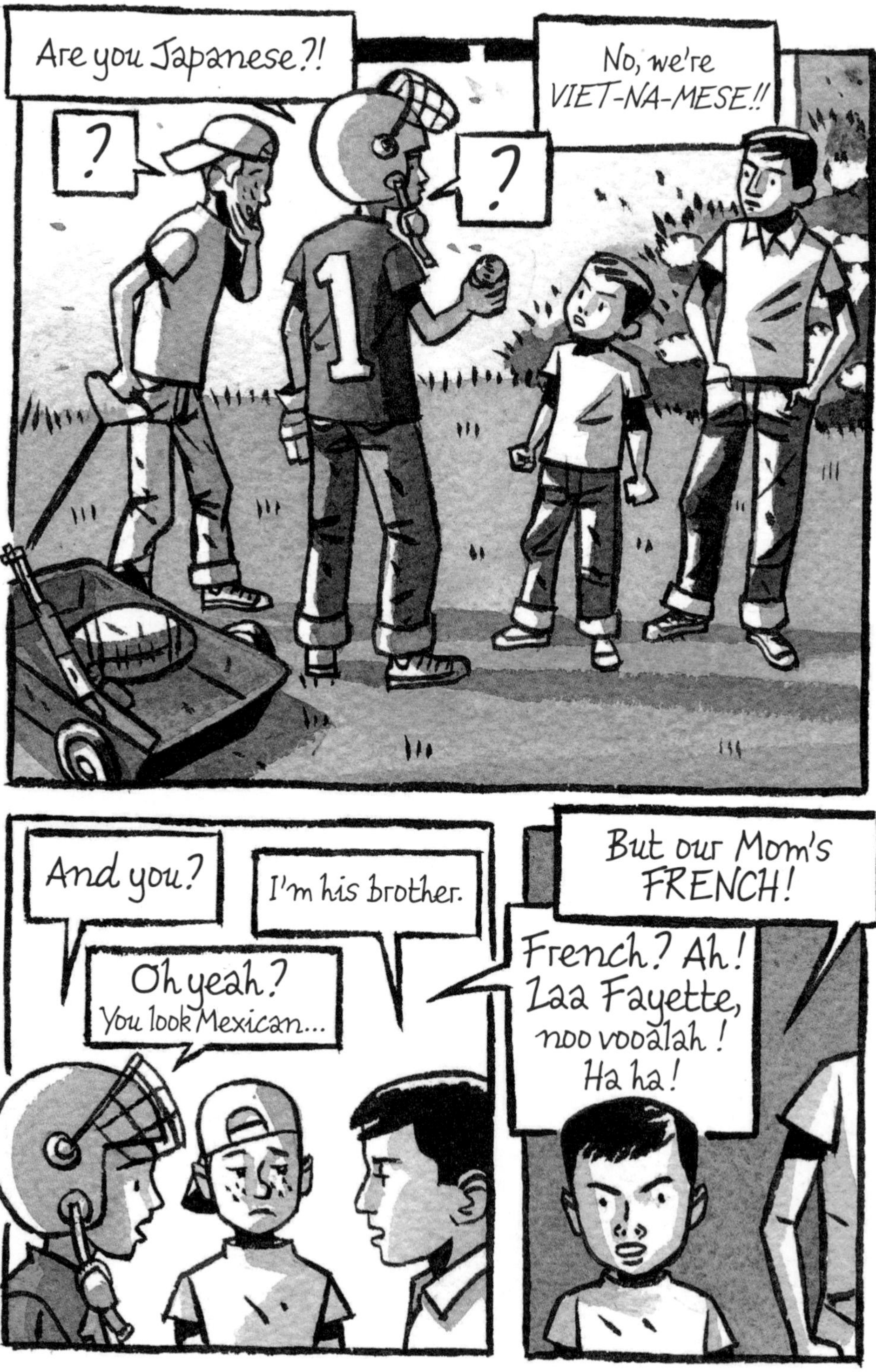
Are you Japanese?!
?
?
No, we're VIET-NA-MESE!!
And you?
I'm his brother.
Oh yeah? You look Mexican...
But our Mom's FRENCH!
French? Ah! Laa Fayette, noo vooalah! Ha ha!

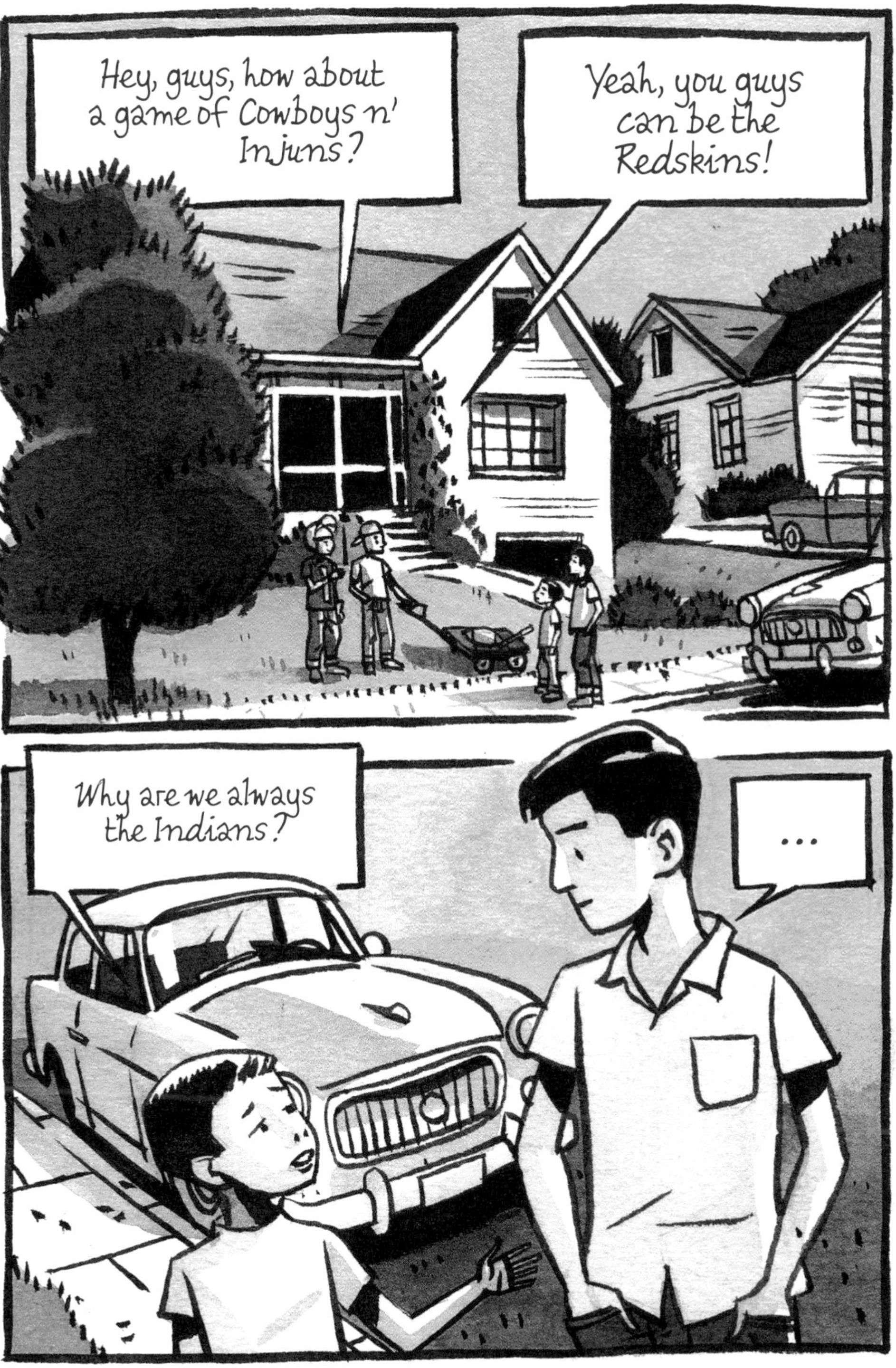
Hey, guys, how about a game of Cowboys n' Injuns?
Yeah, you guys can be the Redskins!
Why are we always the Indians?
...

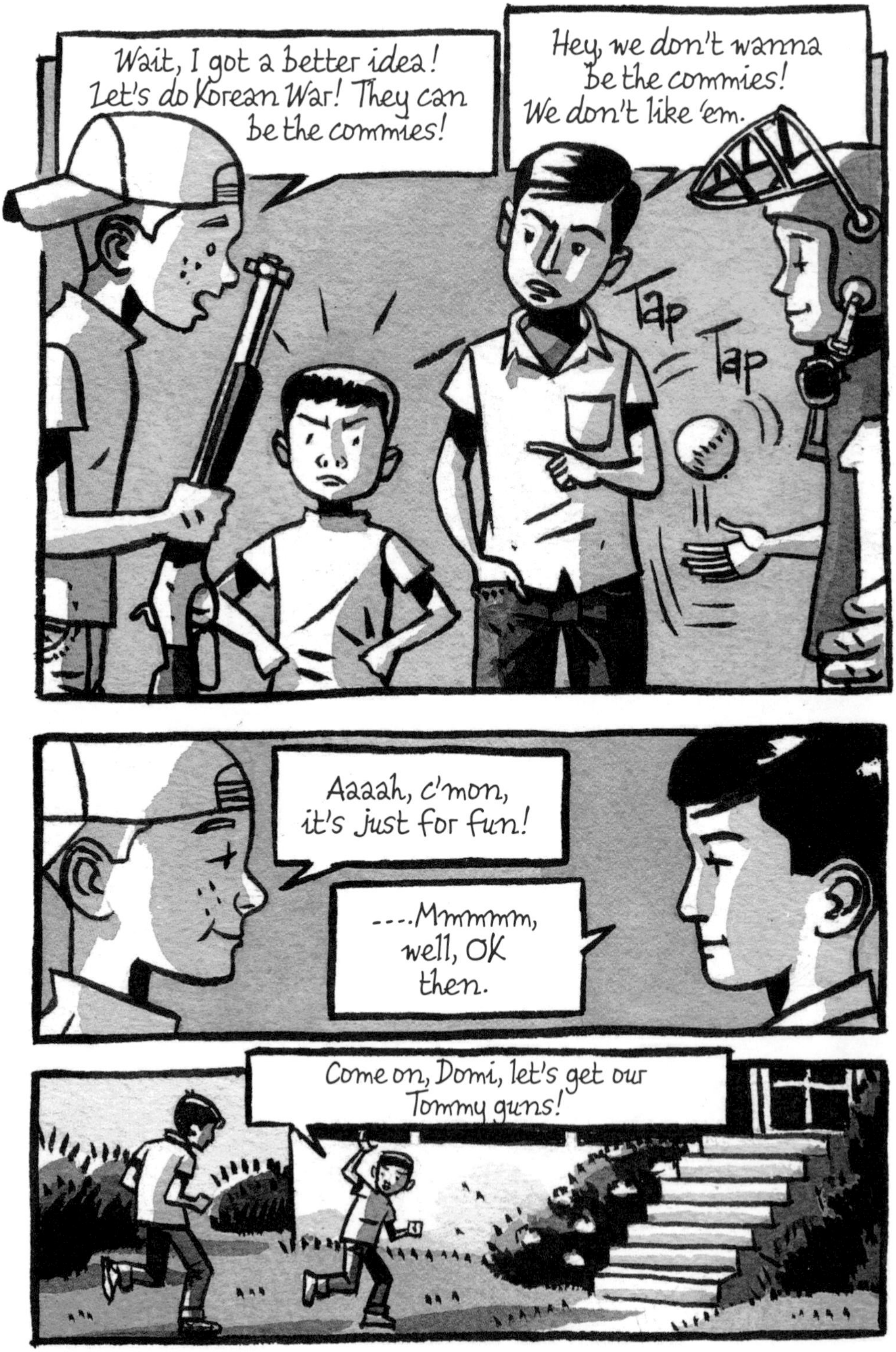
Wait, I got a better idea! Let's do Korean War! They can be the commies!
Hey, we don't wanna be the commies! We don't like 'em.
Tap
Tap
Aaaah, c'mon, it's just for fun!
----Mmmmm, well, OK then.
Come on, Domi, let's get our Tommy guns!

Dear Father and Mother,
We have our share of worries. After I don't know how many false starts, our return to Vietnam has been confirmed. The Ambassador received the letter from the Minister ...

What a change that will be! The children are so happy here, with many friends their age, and they fly from one house to the next like a flock of sparrows.

I am worried sick when I think of all the troubles in Vietnam. Khánh never seems bothered and always says everything will be fine ...

In any case, the prospect of spending a year or two in Saigon is not very appealing, when you can't go any further than a few kilometers out of town, not to mention that I'm not very brave.

Why are you crying, Mama?

It's nothing. I'm writing to Grandpa and Grandma to tell them we have to go back to Vietnam this summer.

Oh...

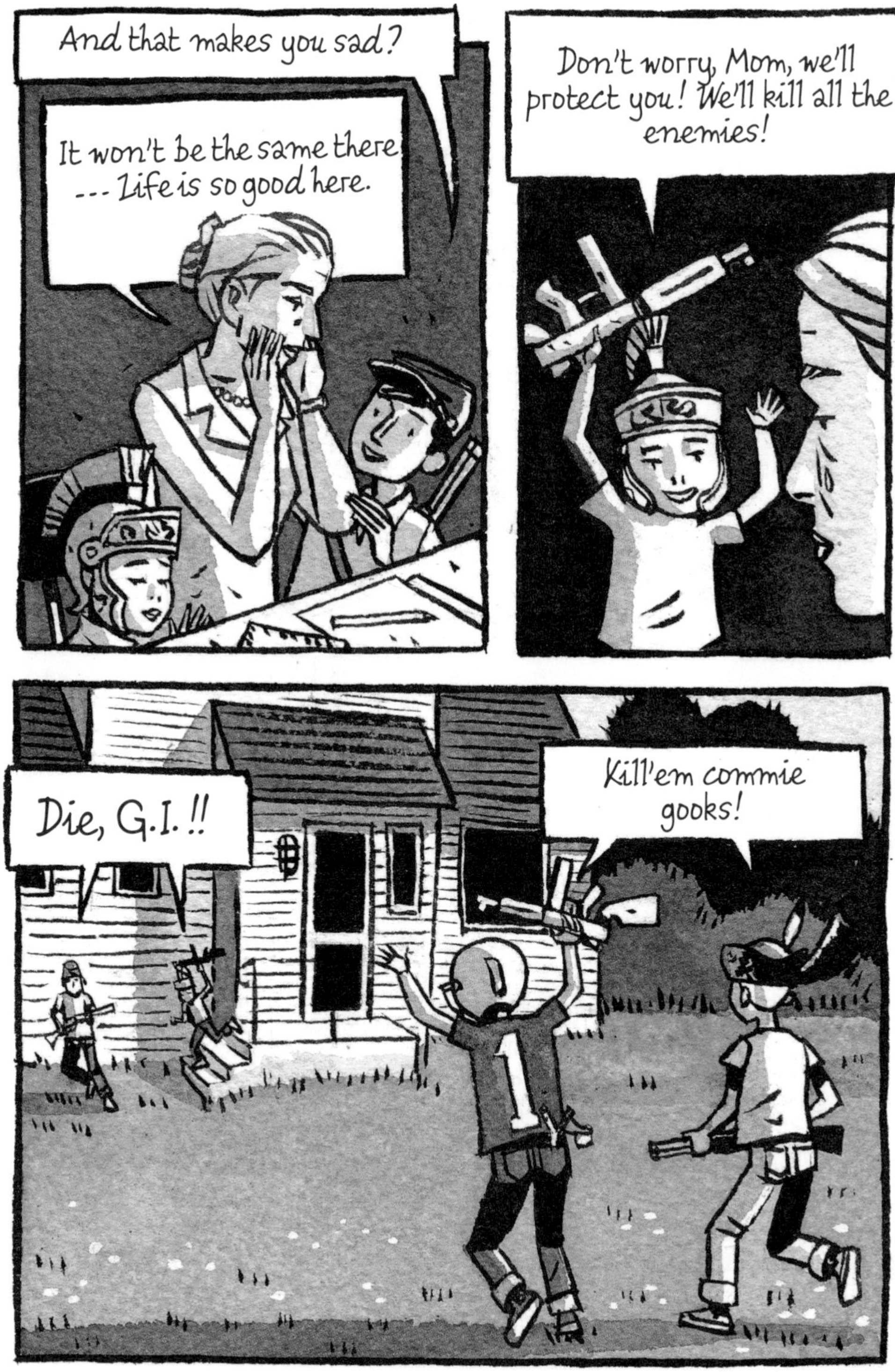
And that makes you sad?
It won't be the same there --- Life is so good here.
Don't worry, Mom, we'll protect you! We'll kill all the enemies!
Die, G.I.!!
Kill'em commie gooks!

We had been living in Washington for three years. Papa was a diplomat at the Vietnamese embassy, and his call back to Saigon sounded the death-knell for Mama's American dream.

No more picnics at Great Falls on the Potomac with the cherry trees in bloom!

Elected in November 1960 over Richard Nixon, President John F. Kennedy moved into the White House in January 1961, and began his 1000-day reign. The young prince took over a nation at the height of its power. JFK wanted this to be the American century.

JFK worked on his image as a Cold War warrior, defying Khrushchev, the Red Tsar, in Cuba and Berlin. But in a country all but unknown to Americans – Vietnam – the real fight was on: Uncle Sam against Uncle Hô!

In his own way, my father participated in the global arm-wrestling. As the cultural attaché at the Vietnamese embassy in Washington, his work was to make Vietnamese culture more widely known, and look after Vietnamese students applying for scholarships in the United States.

France colonized us, but we emancipated ourselves.

I understand.

We Americans had to rid ourselves of the British, you know!

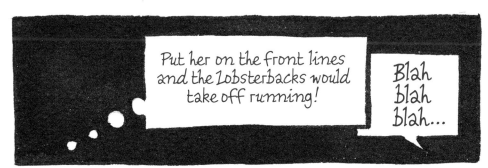

Put her on the front lines and the Lobsterbacks would take off running!

Blah blah blah...

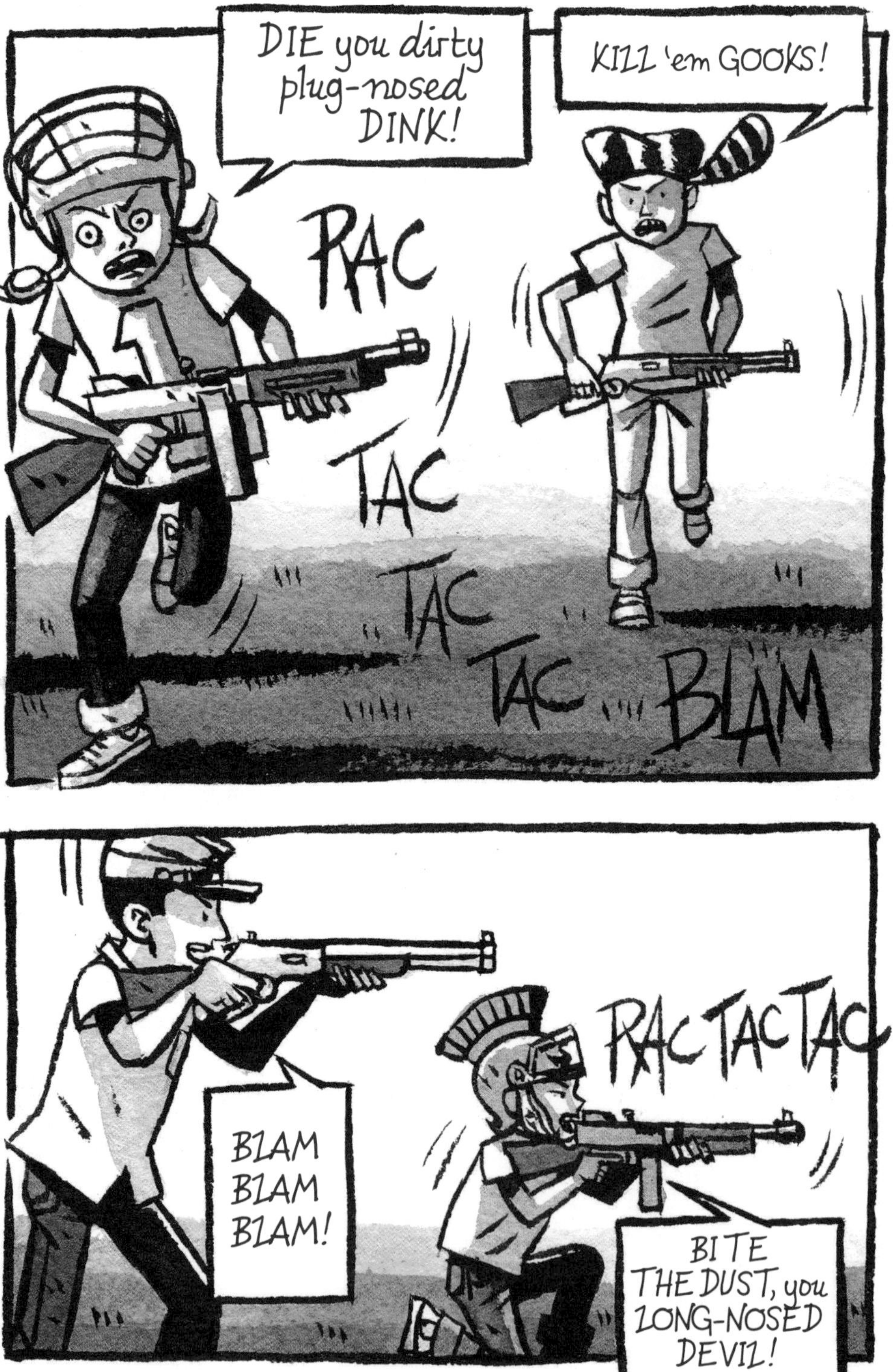
DIE you dirty plug-nosed DINK!
KILL 'em GOOKS!
RAC
TAC
TAC
TAC
BLAM
BLAM BLAM BLAM!
RACTACTAC
BITE THE DUST, you LONG-NOSED DEVIL!

The Hula Hoop was invented in 1958. 100 million of them were sold in 1960.

I remember my first day at kindergarten. Mama at the end of the hallway like a long dark tunnel ---

I got over my pain thanks to a powder you mixed with water: Play-Doh..

Every morning, on the playground, we belted out patriotic songs. "Saluting the colors," it was called.

We went on a field trip to the Gettysburg Battlefield, 90 miles from Washington, the site of great carnage during the Civil War, in 1863.

Washington at Halloween time—an important event—and in winter, sledding in the wet snow ---

--- and American Christmases, with Frank Sinatra crooning ---

--- and sunny souvenirs of Ocean City, a beach in Maryland.

Ocean City was a spot for sport fishing. I remember enormous blue marlin hanging from a gallows.

Before we left for Vietnam, Mama had a bad anxiety attack.

What will happen to us, Khánh? If the Communists take over, they'll massacre all the whites and mixed-race people!

These storms could last hours --- or even days ---

I don't care what your sacrosanct president Diêm* says! He can go to hell!

Please, Yvette --- You're worrying for nothing..

* Ngô Dinh Diêm: the president of the first Republic of Vietnam (1955-1963).

You're mad! Completely unaware!

?!

!

?!

27

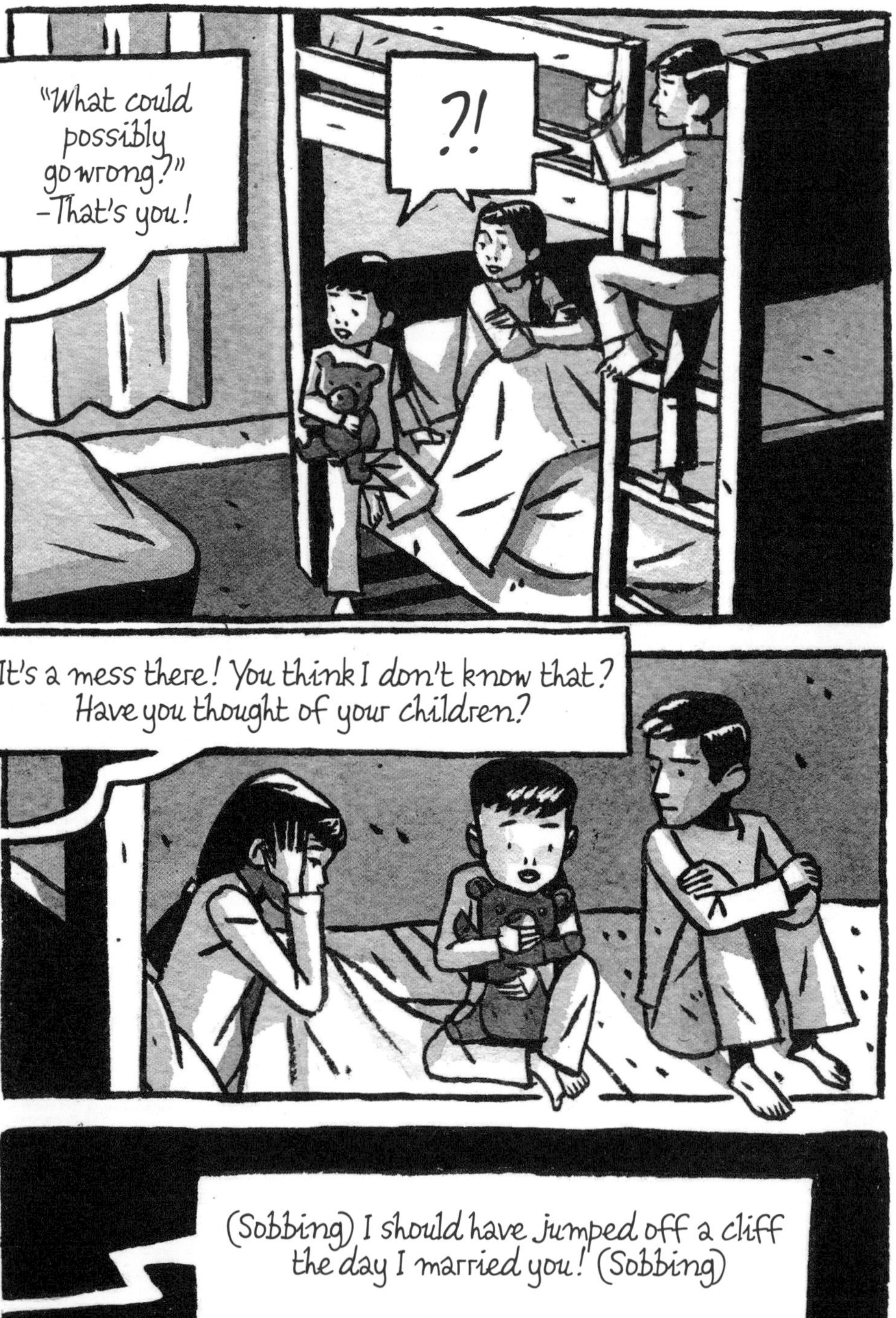
"What could possibly go wrong?" -That's you!
?!
It's a mess there! You think I don't know that? Have you thought of your children?
(Sobbing) I should have jumped off a cliff the day I married you! (Sobbing)

NEW YORK-SAINT-MALO-SAIGON

The moment of truth came in June 1961. Mama was afraid of air travel, so we took the ocean liner SS *Flandre* from New York.

Papa still had work to do. He would join us a few weeks later.

Every morning, to get some time to herself, Mama stuck us in the daycare, which we did not appreciate at all. Strange, but I don't remember much, besides my constant seasickness.

There was one good thing: we saw dolphins!

After six days of sailing, the SS *Flandre* reached Le Havre. Our maternal grandfather was waiting for us.

Our Saint-Malo grandparents were classic French characters right out of a Jacques Tati movie.

My father Victor was a miller. My mother's name was Berthe, like Charlemagne's wife. Big-Foot Berthe.*

Big-Foot Berthe? Ha ha!

Is the watering can too heavy, Grandma?

Oh, you know, I grew up in the country, Mireille.

VROOM VROOM

Grandpa had a Normandy accent and rolled his "r's." He loved spending time in his workshop, a Gauloise in his mouth, where he made us toys out of wood.

Marrrco, can you give me the wood file?

* Apparently, Berthe had a clubfoot.

Our grandmother Denise had been an exceptional schoolteacher. She kept instructing us wherever we were.

Between us, we spoke English most of the time.

Grandpa took us on long walks along the walls of the old town that was just being rebuilt.

Saint-Malo was still an active harbor with its sailors' district, the rue de la Soif.

Aunt Annie, Mama's sister, visited us with her husband Guy, who was also my godfather.

A merchant marine officer, he had served his two years service in Algeria as an ensign in the French Navy commandos. Bitterness was written on his face. The radio brought news of Kennedy in Berlin, but also of the Algiers putsch and the OAS.

35

Papa finally met up with us in France and in July 1961, we took the Air France flight from Paris to Saigon.

Wow! Is that a Caramel?
Silly Billy! It's a Caravelle! Ha ha!

A 16-hour flight, with stops in Athens, Tehran ---

Ha ha!

Mireille, Domi, I didn't run to Iran, I flew! In a Caramel!

Very funny! Ha ha!

--- Karachi, and Bangkok.

ZZZZ

Did you see his hat?

He's from Pakistan.

The flight from Bangkok to Saigon was very difficult. A violent monsoon storm was raging over Southeast Asia.

The dark sky seemed angry. Mama was livid.

We flew right into the turbulence ---

In 1954, after a hundred years of colonial domination and seven years of war with France, Vietnam won its independence.

The Communists triumphed at Diên Biên Phu. But not all Vietnamese were on their side. Some had fought alongside the French for a non-Communist Vietnam. And many were undecided. The 1954 Geneva Accords that put an end to the war in Indochina attempted to take these divisions into consideration.

*Victory!

To separate the former belli-
gerents, Vietnam was tempo-
rarily divided in two. In the
North, a Communist state with
Hanoi as its capital. In the
South, a nationalist state with
Saigon as its capital. According to the peace treaty, general elections were to be held
in 1956 to decide which political system would govern the
country after reunification:
Communist or nationalist.

North Vietnam
became a people's
republic along
Chinese lines.
The old militant
of international
Communism, Hô
Chi Minh—Uncle
Hô—ran an
iron-clad regime,
forged in war.

The strongman
from the South was
Ngô Dinh Diêm,
a Catholic and
ardent nationalist.
A protégé of the
Americans, he
was named prime
minister during the
Geneva Conference.

39

From 1954 on, a million people from North Vietnam, mostly Catholics, headed southward to flee the Communist regime. We now know that CIA agents whipped up fear of the Reds.

Meanwhile, 90000 soldiers who had fought the French in South Vietnam with the Communist army—the Viêt Minh—moved North, abandoning their families, convinced they would be returning home in two years, after the general elections. It was true that Communist leader Hô Chi Minh, wearing the halo of victory, was expected to win by most observers.

In 1955, the North carried out land reform, emulating the Russian and Chinese models. In a mockery of justice, 15000 landowners were executed. Peasant revolts broke out and 50000 peasants were put to death. By the end of 1956, Hô Chi Minh politely admitted that his land reform had gone too far.

In the South, two years later, Ngô Dinh Diêm toppled Emperor Bao Dai, declared his country a republic, fought opponents on all sides, and established a semblance of order, but refused to hold the general elections set for 1956.

Denis Warner,
Australian journalist

An interpreter

President Diêm

A confirmed bachelor, Diêm was supported by his clan of five brothers. The eldest had been murdered by the Viêt Minh. The second, Thuc, was a bishop, and the younger ones, Cân and Luyên, were a provincial governor and an ambassador, respectively. The most influential—Ngô Dinh Nhu—was Diêm's personal advisor and political mentor, or so people said.

To fight Communist subversion, Nhu advised using Hanoi's methods: a secret police force and an iron fist. The regime's éminence grise, he contributed to its hard line.

We must close the nightclubs and dance-halls!

For the Communists, the end justifies the means.

His wife, Madame Nhu, acted as the regime's first lady. Her feminine wiles and outrageous declarations made her the darling of the foreign press. *Life* and *Paris Match* adored the character she played.

In 1959, the Communist insurrection* started again in the South. Small bands dug up the guns hidden in 1954. They murdered government employees to destabilize the Saigon regime. They attacked military installations and captured weapons.

Aim carefully, every cartridge counts!

RAC TAC TAC

The repression was merciless. Communists were hunted down in the South. A guillotine made the rounds of the countryside.

Where did you hide your guns?

At the end of '59, Hanoi decided to take up armed struggle again by infiltrating the South with former Viêt Minh fighters who had been regrouped in the North between 1954 and 1956. Men and weapons were sent southward by sea and the Hô Chi Minh Trail, a network of footpaths crossing the wild landscapes of Laos and Cambodia.

* The Communists called it "the Resistance."

In 1960, the National Liberation Front (NLF) was created in the South. This clandestine movement insisted it was independent of Hanoi. That posturing didn't impress the Saigon regime, which bestowed the pejorative name "Viêt Cong" on it, or Vietnamese Communist.

But not all NLF fighters were Communists. Many were simply fervent patriots who fought and died by the tens of thousands. There were so many women fighting on the front lines that it was said they formed their own "long-haired army."

In 1961, only 40% of South Vietnam's territory was controlled by the government. Some areas, known as "liberated zones," were considered off-limits by Saigon's forces.

The US had always supported the anti-Communist side, but John Kennedy, when he became president, boosted the aid considerably.

He sent weapons ---

--- and advisors, so no one would have to read the instruction manuals ---

--- and as always, the population was caught between a rock and a hard place.

This civil war (a notion challenged by the Communists who considered all opposition the work of a foreign power) produced a thousand violent deaths every month.

45

And that was the worrisome situation in Saigon when we showed up in July 1961 ---

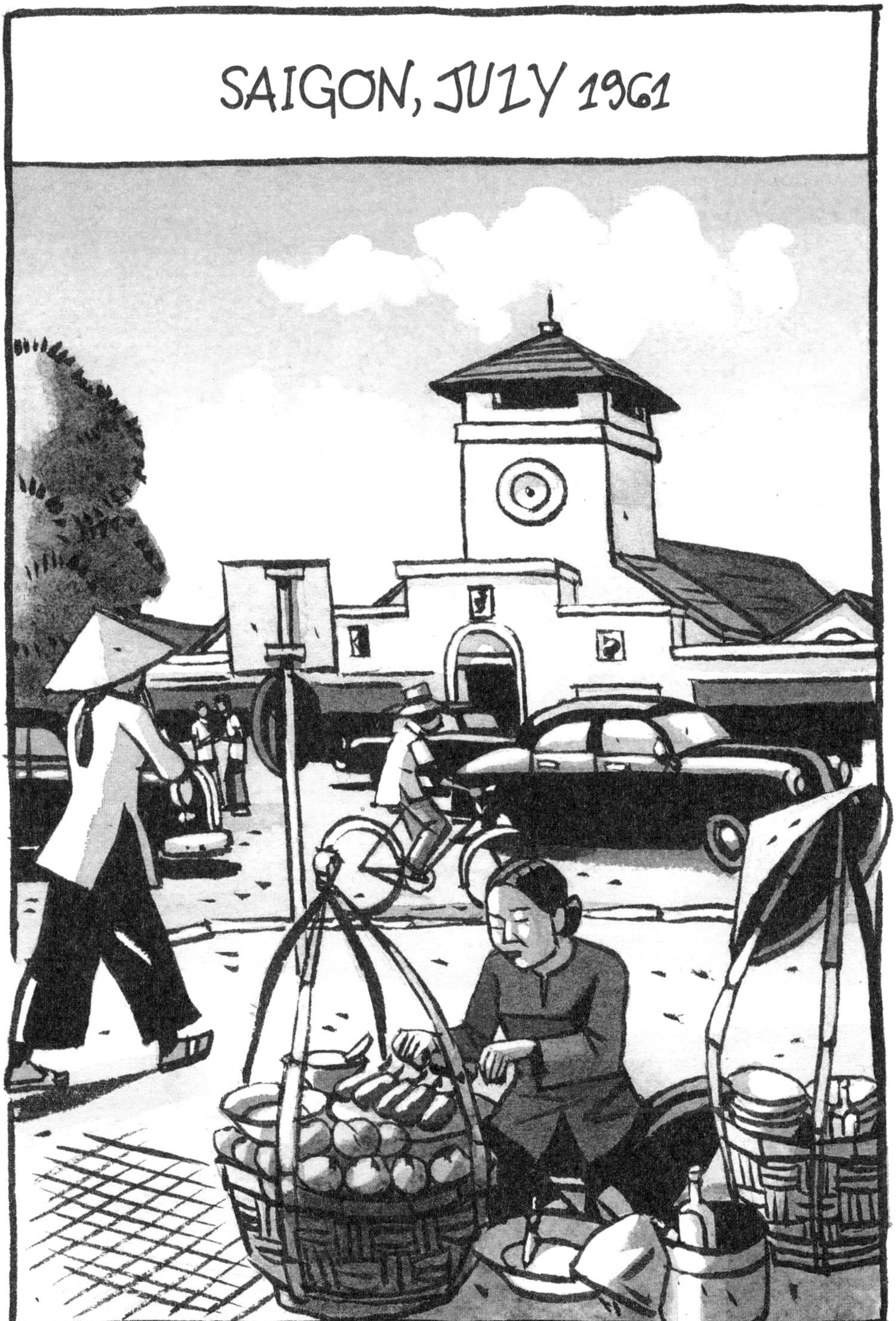
SAIGON, JULY 1961

Despite the rain, the moist heat stuck to our skin.

Our Uncle Lâm was a history professor and researcher, and he borrowed the History Museum's minibus.

Until we found a place to live, we would be staying with Papa's parents in Gia-Dinh, a Saigon suburb.

* How are things going now?

* It's quiet, but that could change ⋯

In November 1960, a group of paratroopers attempted a putsch that threatened the Saigon regime. The event left 400 dead and shook the President's confidence in his elite units.

* **Ông Nội:** paternal grandfather   **Bà Nội:** paternal grandmother

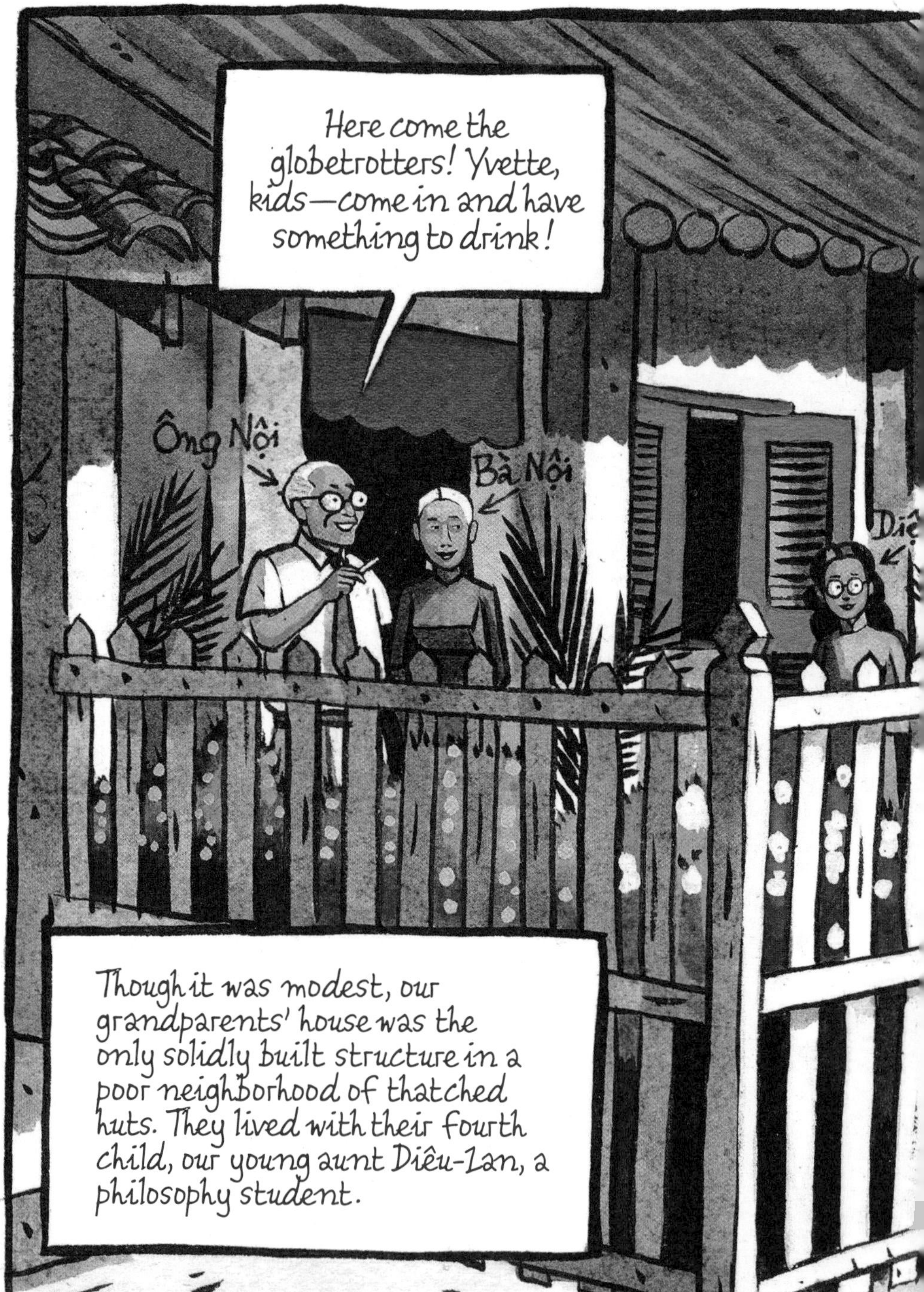
Here come the globetrotters! Yvette, kids—come in and have something to drink!
Ông Nội
Bà Nội
Though it was modest, our grandparents' house was the only solidly built structure in a poor neighborhood of thatched huts. They lived with their fourth child, our young aunt Diêu-Lan, a philosophy student.

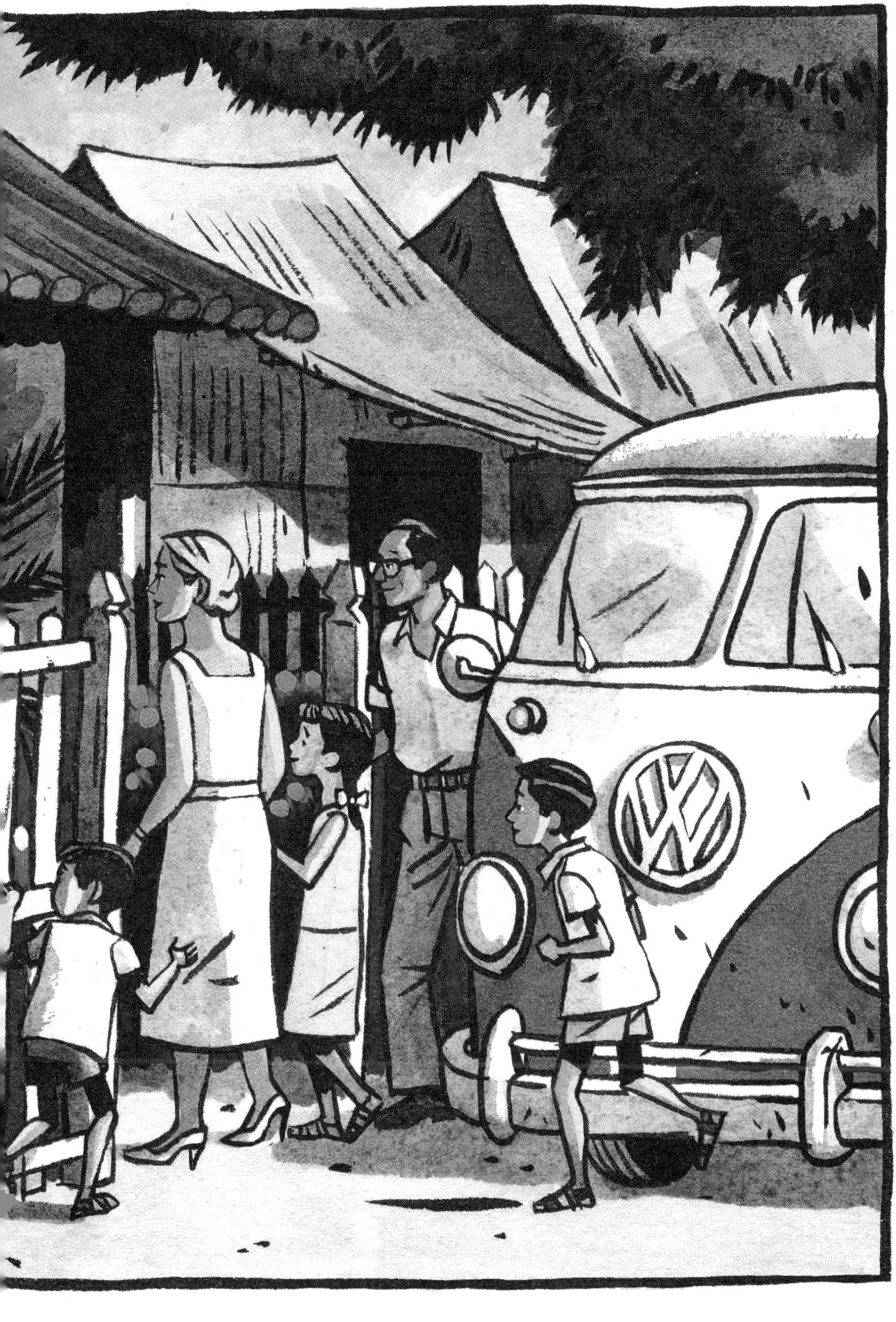

Our Saigon grandpa was easy-going, and he soon conquered us.

Ông Nôi has a jelly belly! Ha Ha!

A swelly belly that shakes like Jelly!

Ha! Ha! I'm going to water your flowers, Grandpa!

That's very nice, Mireille!

Bà Nôi communicated through feelings and food.
Every day, new dishes awaited us.

This is good! What is it, Domi?

<Munch, munch> Five-spice pork belly!!

You're so stupid, Marco!

Jelly belly?! Like Ông Nôi's?! Ha ha!!

With them, we discovered some of Saigon's pleasures: ice cream at Givral's, and the books at the Portail bookstore.

Papa's new job wasn't defined yet, but often President Diêm called him to the Independence Palace when he needed an interpreter. Most of the time, the President phoned himself.

DRING
DRING

Papa, telephone!

Hello?

À, Anh Khánh hỉ? Anh có thể đến dinh Độc lập 6 giờ ngày mai không? *

* Ah, Khánh. Can you come to the Palace tomorrow morning at six?

Vâng. Thưa Ông Tổng Thống, được! *

Ông Tổng Thống?

«Ông Tổng Thống! Ông Tổng Thống!!»

Bà Nội

Ông Nội

* Yes, Mr. President, of course.

56

Papa looked for a house in the center of the city because our grandparents said their suburb wasn't safe at night. Papa's other brother, Uncle Diên, said there was a free apartment in his building.

An American couple was living there but they just left.

Is the security good?

Yes! The building is guarded night and day. Our brother Lâm lives there too.

Điên →

Mama, as she used to say, was "worried sick."

We're going to live in a building with your whole tribe?

They're eager to be of service. They'll help us settle in.!

Mama's worrying sometimes soured her view of life.

Sometimes we overheard our parents' discussions.

At night, geckos and crickets provided the sound track for our dreams and nightmares.

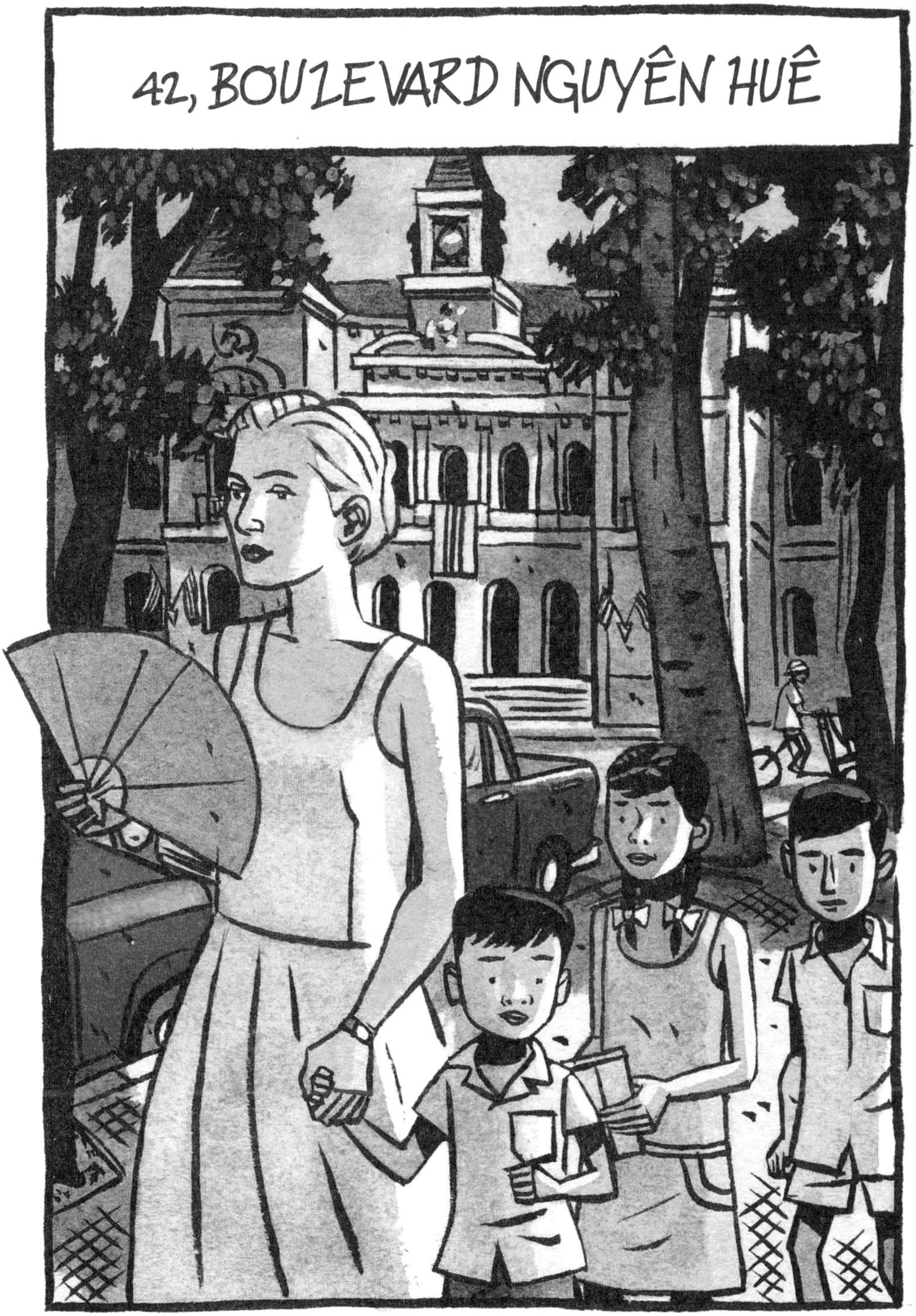
42, BOULEVARD NGUYÊN HUÊ

In August, we moved to the sixth floor of a new building at 42 Boulevard Nguyễn Huê, right in the middle of the city.

Our apartment

One thing surprised us following our move from the US: there was no glass in the windows because it was warm all the time. Big blinds and shutters protected us from the sun and rain.

Look, you can see City Hall!

Those Americans have got their nerve!

They took the air conditioner with them!

Ick, there's a spider web!

U.S. GO HOME! Ha ha!

Good Lord, look at this dust.

Only our parents' room had air conditioning.

It's too hot! I can't sleep!

Me neither!

And there's a mosquito too!

BZZZZ BZZZZ

In our room, the fan stirred the air like a spoon in a boiling cauldron.

To help Mama, a 17-year-old girl, Chi Hai, was hired. Mama tried to teach the maid, as they were called back then, the mysteries of French cooking.

* You don't put nuoc-mam (fish sauce) in boeuf bourguignon.

We went to school in the morning. At recess, we didn't understand a thing, since most kids spoke Vietnamese.
At home, we spoke French.

* You want to play with me? What's your name?

Every afternoon, after our nap, Mother *did* her own schooling, since she was appalled at how poorly we were doing. She truly was a schoolteacher's daughter.

You don't hold a fountain pen that way! What a nitwit!*

That's because in America, we wrote with Bic pens!

And Domi prefers to draw!

* This was when it was still common for parents to say such things to their child

In an August 1961 letter sent to our grandparents in France, Mother enclosed Domi's drawing. He was 8 years old.

A missile, a threatening flying machine, cars and buildings every which way --- Domi asked Mama to write on the drawing, upside down, "Are you CACAHUÈTE?" "Cacahuète" in French means "peanut," but the accent was on the NUTS—as in crazy. Did Domi sense the madness gathering over Saigon and our family?

63

When four o'clock came, Mother often took us to the little park in front of the National Assembly, the former Lyric Theater from the French era. Mireille was learning the La Fontaine fable "The Town Rat and the Country Rat" at the Lamartine School.

"A city rat, upon a day, Invited from his curds..."

You needn't remind us, Marco!

Poor people eat rats here!

Ick!

Our mother's blonde hair attracted a lot of attention ...

Bà Đầm!*

Ick, that's horrible! No fingers, and no nose!

!?

My God, a leper! Quick, let's go home!

* Madame!

In the vain quest for cooler air, we would often stroll along the Bach Dang pier, a few steps from our building.

Every day, Papa went to the Independence Palace, since President Diêm needed an interpreter's help for discussions with English-speaking visitors. This woman is Dickey Chapelle, a photographer who was later killed in 1965 during a military operation.*

After a while, Papa was named director of "Agence Vietnam-Presse." They announced his appointment in the paper.

One day in October, we got some surprising news.

Look how handsome our Papa is!

You're going to have a little brother or a little sister!

In January, there will be one more of us!

?!

* Dickey Chapelle was the first woman war correspondent to die in Vietnam, during Operation Black Ferret.

66

PROJECT BEEF-UP

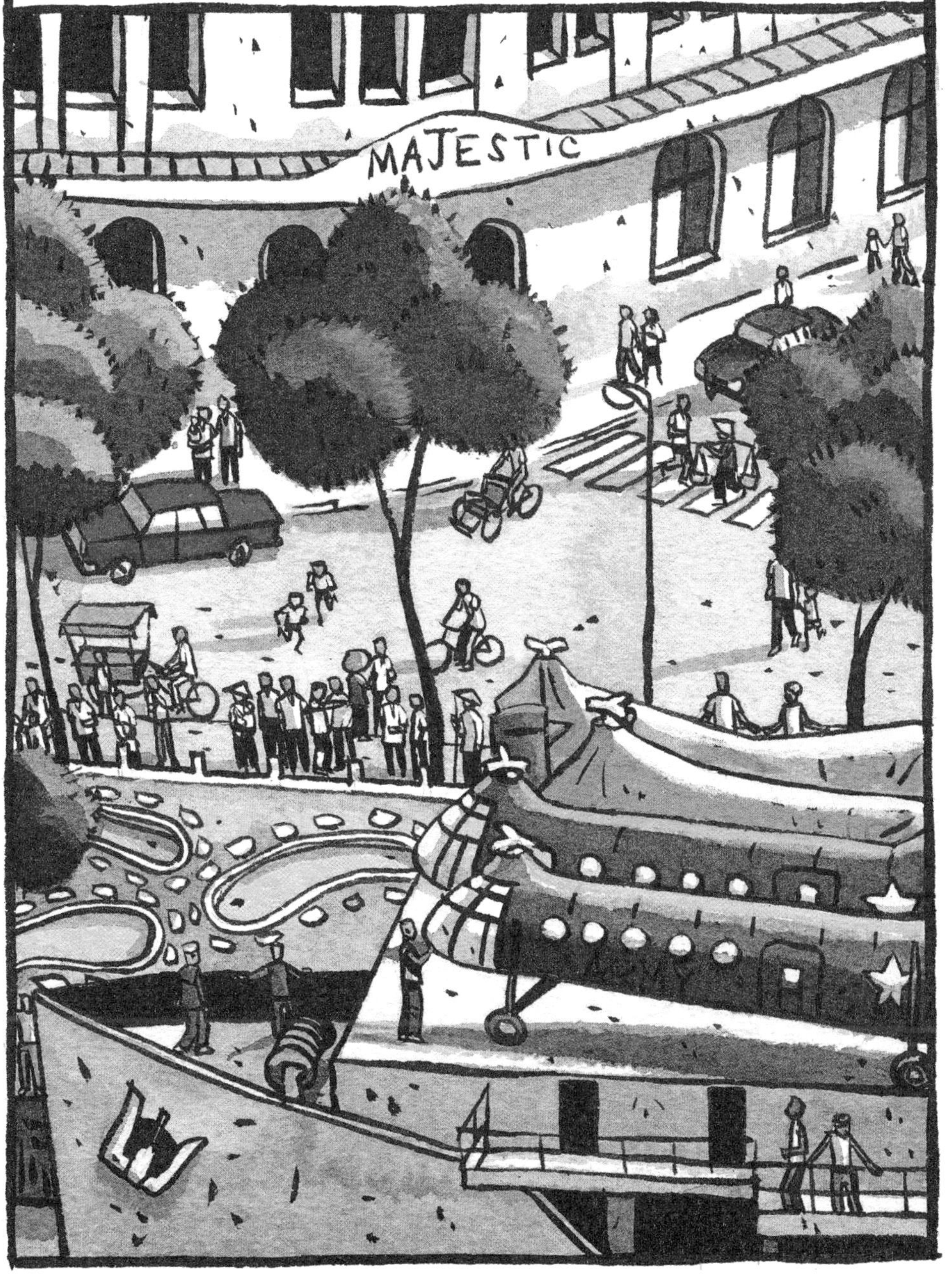
MAJESTIC

Mama wrote regular letters to her parents in France, and they kept every one. Thanks to those letters, fifty years later I could reconstruct our daily life. In October 1961, things were going badly ---

"Don't worry, my pregnancy is just fine, but I'm getting the jitters, since a state of emergency was declared, and with it, a general call-up. I was in a state because Khánh could have been drafted, but he was judged indispensable because of his job, and he wasn't in danger. But we're afraid of attacks, and the streets are full of soldiers ..."

Khánh, do you think there will be war? Do you think the North Vietnamese will invade the South?

Of course not, Yvette! We took measures to instill fear in the Communists ---

At the end of October, with Mama tired because of her pregnancy, a second "servant" was recruited.

Bong jou' Badam' Khanh!

Ah, Chu Ba*?

Chu Ba was sent by Aunt Elvira, who lived on the ninth floor.

Yvette, I'm giving you Chu Ba, I can't stand him anymore.

* Chu Ba: Third Uncle. Pronounced "Teoo Ba."

Elvira was a Latvian with defi-nite Slavic charm. Our Uncle Lâm met her when he was a student in Belgium.

I hope he knows how to work.

The men here are so lazy!

Chu Ba's main task was to drive our Rambler through the chaotic streets of Saigon.

Chu Ba is a great driver!

Yeah!

Mireille, Domi! Đây là trường Lamartine!*

* Here's the Lamartine School!

I liked to go with Mama when she went visiting Elvira. I was very aware of the charm and beauty of the two women.

Our Uncle Lâm was the director of the Institute of Historical Research. Elvira and he had exquisite taste and their house was a regular museum ---

Their high-heeled shoes awoke secret desires in me.

Since Mama had to have complete bed rest, we headed into the great steam bath of Saigon with Chu Ba.

"Ya Mustapha," the hit by the Lebanese singer Bob Azzam, was on everyone's lips. The Vietnamese loved bursting into song.

* Do you want to have some pho, kids?

To escape the heat, the privileged classes repaired to the swimming pool at the Cercle Sportif de Saigon, a pure 1930s-style installation, located in a park behind the Independence Palace.

* I have a swimming class with Monsieur Vatin at 5.

Chu Ba never went swimming. He was happy watching us and sipping a lemonade, which was the Cercle's specialty.

It was hot, and in the coral trees in the park, hundreds of cicadas whirred away, loud but invisible ---

Aunt Elvira was often there, soaking up the sun. I watched for her smile, her blonde hair and gray eyes.

By the pool, the war was nowhere to be found. Though sometimes it flew past ---

They say the Viêt-Cong have underground bases less than 50 km from Saigon!

Nothin' to worry about, lady! Slopes can't shoot straight.

Look, Domi, warplanes!

Wow! Those are Skyraiders!

* The Douglas Skyraider: an American fighter-bomber. The emblematic plane of the Vietnam War.

Photos of Viêt-Cong attacks filled the newspapers and fascinated me.

* Come on, kids, let's go!

75

One day In December 1961, I was out walking with Chu Ba when an enormous American aircraft carrier sailed into view. The USC V* Core was delivering Kennedy's Christmas gift to our door: sophisticated ---

*United States Carrier Vessel

--- armaments to add muscle to our army. An aid plan called "Project Beef-Up." The "banana" helicopters in their protective wrapping looked like strange chrysalises.

Helicopters were considered the panacea when it came to fighting guerrillas. Our American advisors had studied in Algeria with the French paratroopers who successfully used choppers against the rebels.

Mama commented on the events in a letter to her parents dated December 9, 1961: "An aircraft carrier arrived in Saigon. American forces have been deployed (40 helicopters) in the heart of the city. The crowds are very proud. There are a few American soldiers as well. On the Vietnamese side, trucks full of well-equipped soldiers can be seen. The same joie de vivre as before. And such busy streets!"

The USCV *Core* kept rotating, delivering all the ultra-nasty machinery: choppers, armored vehicles, airplanes --- Here's a drawing I made, dated April 1962.

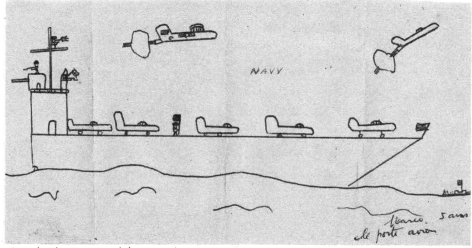

* Look, Chu Ba, a tank!

CHRISTMAS 1961 & TÊT 1962

* Têt : Vietnamese new year.

As Christmas drew near, the stores filled with cheap toys from Hong Kong. Nguyên Huê Boulevard was known for its florists, and it was brimming over with flowers and even Christmas trees—real and artificial.

Let's look at the toys, Marco, ok?

Sure. I saw a toy tank!

The heat kept building and Mama, 7 months pregnant, became more anxious.

I wonder if Mama's going to yell at Chi Hai,* Chu Ba, or Papa.

She's no fun when she gets wound up!

* The girl who cooked for us.

80

Tormented by her anxieties, Mama wrote to her parents and confided her fear of having to "give birth in a horrible hospital like the one in 'Gone with the Wind.'" Around that time, Chu Ba's wife brought her fifth child into the world ---

Here's what Mama said about it:

"Chu Ba's wife had her baby at the public lying-in hospital. The child (her 5th) was a breach birth. Three doctors were looking after her, just how well, I don't know. The second evening, she was sent home after a transfusion, since the public hospital had no more room for her. Her husband Chu Ba had to pay in kind by giving two liters of blood (which seems enormous to me)."

January 1962. The heat was oppressive. At night, the sheets seemed to be on fire---

Before turning off the light, we hunted mosquitoes.

I loved the noise of Saigon. Horns, sputtering motorbikes, the calls of the itinerant vendors ---

* Who wants grilled cuttlefish?

82

Just like Vietnamese children, we raised crickets that we found in the air ducts, where they lived alongside enormous cockroaches.

Each of us had a champion living in a matchbox.

Some crickets were natural fighters. Others were singers, and even if we pushed them into the ring with a hair, they wouldn't react. Pacifists ---

Crooners and gladiators were dressed in the same black armor. They were the miners of the air ducts, and their smooth round heads shone like boxing gloves.

At the end of January 1962, our sister Anh-Noëlle (Christmas Light) came into the world at the Hôpital Grall, a French hospital.

Your little sister is adorable!

And Mama is doing fine.

We'll have to behave when Mama comes back. She'll be tired!

Anh-Noëlle's birth changed the family dynamic ---

I won't be the baby anymore.

She really is cute, Mama!

Sweet enough to eat!

Every Monday morning, loudspeakers all across Saigon belted out a hymn to President Ngô Đình Diệm.

Our building

♪♫ Ngô Tổng Thống, Ngô Tổng Thống muôn năm! ♫♪*

* May President Ngô reign ten thousand years!

Which was Saigon's attempt to imitate the cult of personality fervently practiced in the North.

♫ Chủ Tịch Hồ Chí Minh muôn năm!*♫♪

* May President Hồ Chí Minh reign for ten thousand years!

85

One Monday, as the hymn to President Ngô echoed through the streets ---

♪ Ngô Tổng Thống   Ngô Tổng Thống muôn năm!

Good God!

Aba Aba!

Anna* cried again last night.

Sure, but she's just a baby.

* Anna is Anh-Noëlle

I can't stand their Tổng Thống anymore!

Danh bạ điện thoại Sài-Gòn.

Aba Aba!

Telephone book

To hell with Tổng Thống!

!   !

Aba Aba!

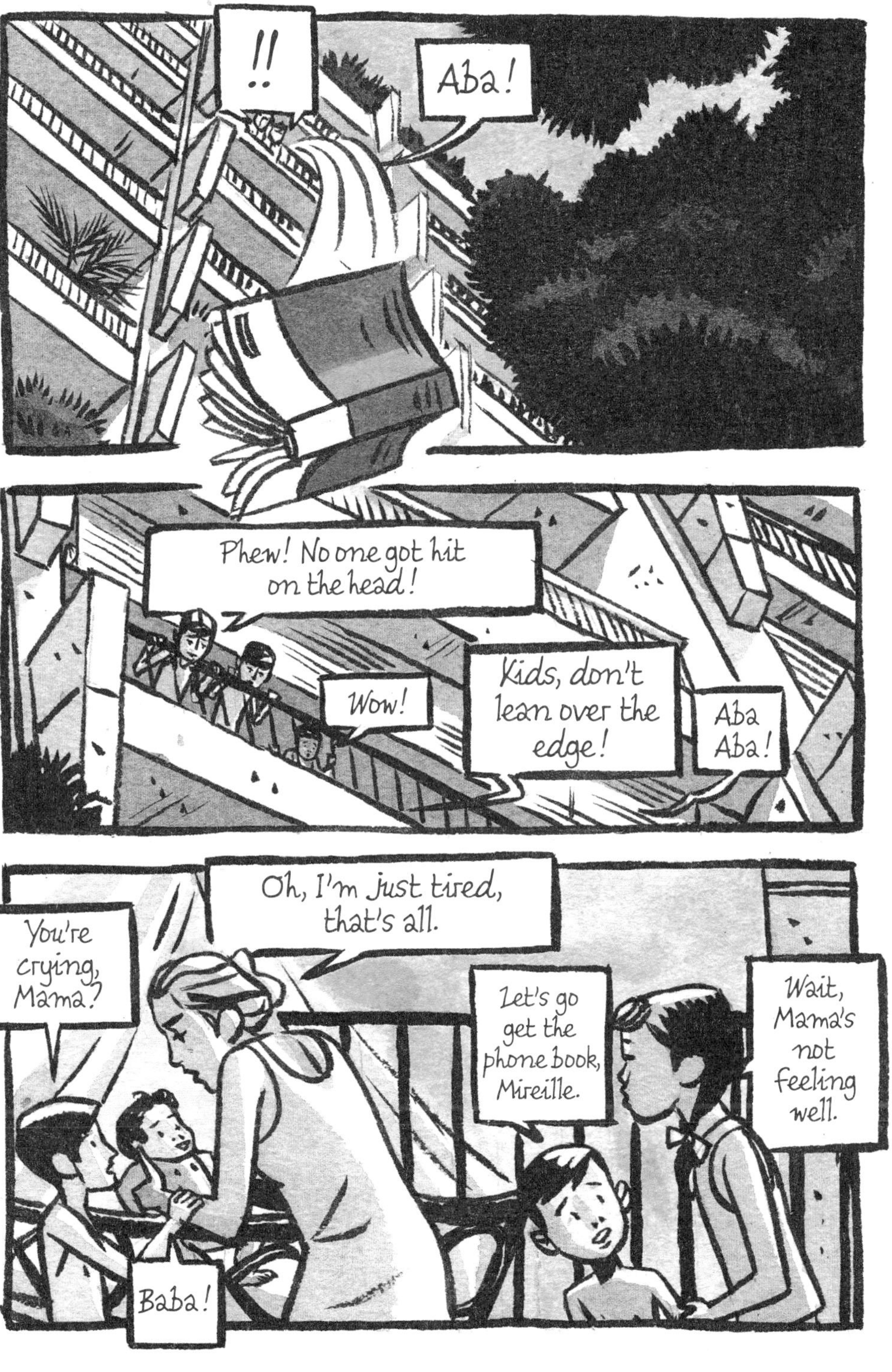
!!
Aba!
Phew! No one got hit on the head!
Wow!
Kids, don't lean over the edge!
Aba Aba!
You're crying, Mama?
Oh, I'm just tired, that's all.
Let's go get the phone book, Mireille.
Wait, Mama's not feeling well.
Baba!

A few weeks after giving birth, happy to have lost weight, Mama felt better and began going to receptions with Papa.

Society life continued, even if news of the war was bad.
The Viêt-Cong attacks grew ever bolder.

US M1 Garand rifle

Faced with the Viêt-Cong offensive, some officers of the Saigon army simply called in air strikes or used artillery, concerned only with protecting themselves.

Requesting air support. I repeat! Requesting air support!

RAC TAC TAC

RAC TAC TAC TAC

Unfortunately, these tactics produced innocent victims, providing the NLF with new recruits eager for vengeance.

Trời đất ơi! Trời ơi! *

* Heaven and earth!

Officially, American advisors didn't take part in combat. But in the field, things were different. Kennedy's boys got their hands dirty and couldn't wait to take over the fight.

Take this, gook-face!

RAC TAC TAC TAC TAC

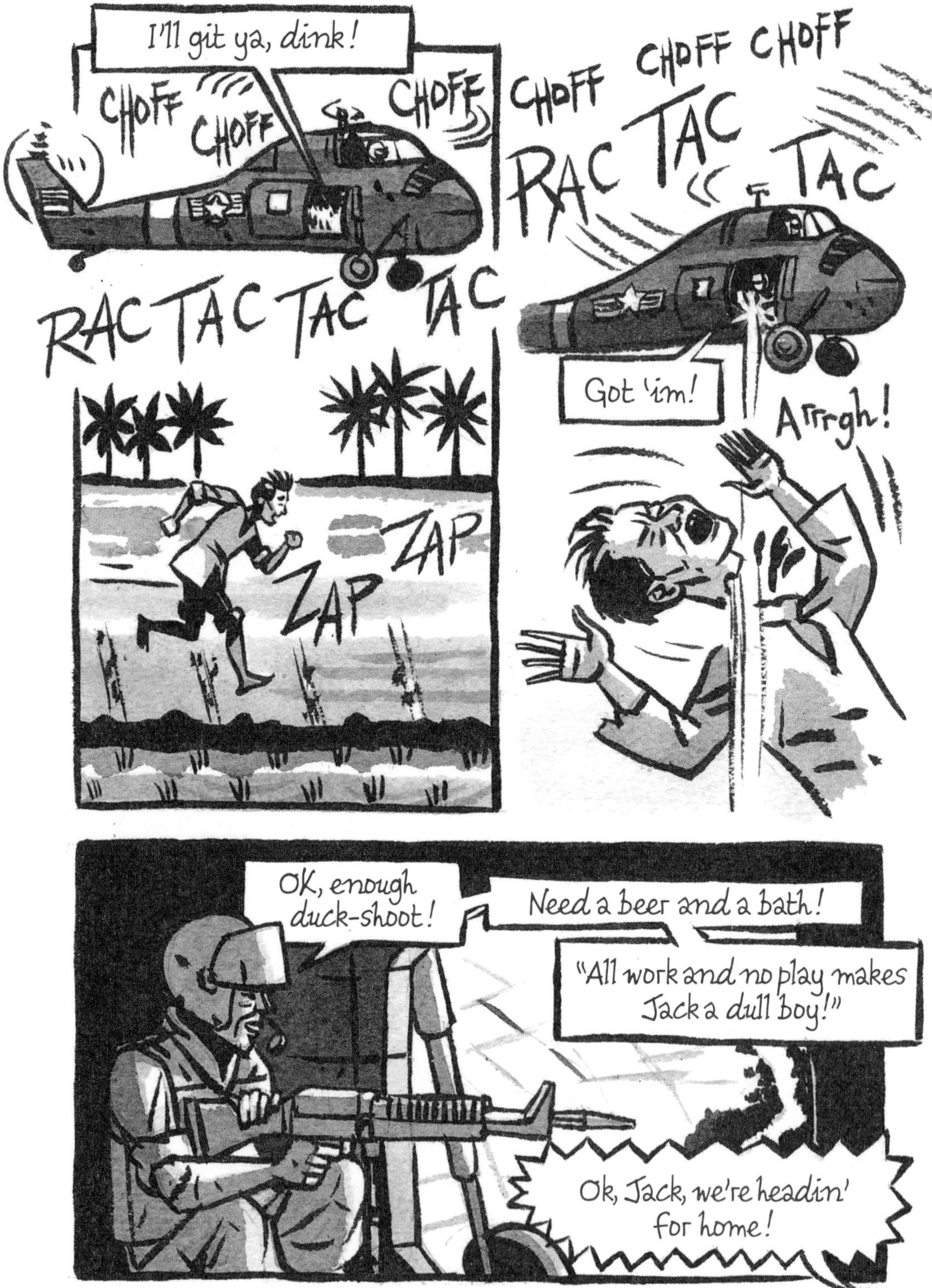
I'll git ya, dink!
CHOFF
CHOFF
CHOFF
RAC TAC TAC TAC
CHOFF CHOFF CHOFF
RAC TAC TAC
Got 'im!
ZAP
ZAP
Arrrgh!
OK, enough duck-shoot!
Need a beer and a bath!
"All work and no play makes Jack a dull boy!"
Ok, Jack, we're headin' for home!

The dirty war raged in the countryside. In town, the social niceties continued unabated.

Shall we dance, Khánh?

You know I don't know how to dance, Yvette.

Uhh--- Mr. Khánh?

♪ Dancing in the dark, 'til the tune ends... ♪

Oh, no, not another boring guy!

Yes?

I'm Neil Sheehan, UPI. Tomorrow I'm heading for the delta with your boys.

Don't be too quick to judge. Our cause is just, even though sometimes we may look like the bad guys.

Would you like to dance, Madame Khánh?

With pleasure, Mr. Ambassador!

For the reporters of the time, it was still a lovely little war, with just enough adrenaline. To see it, you showed up at dawn at the Saigon airport.

The mayor and the teacher in a village near Tra Vinh were assassinated. We suspect the village is friendly to the Viêt-Cong.

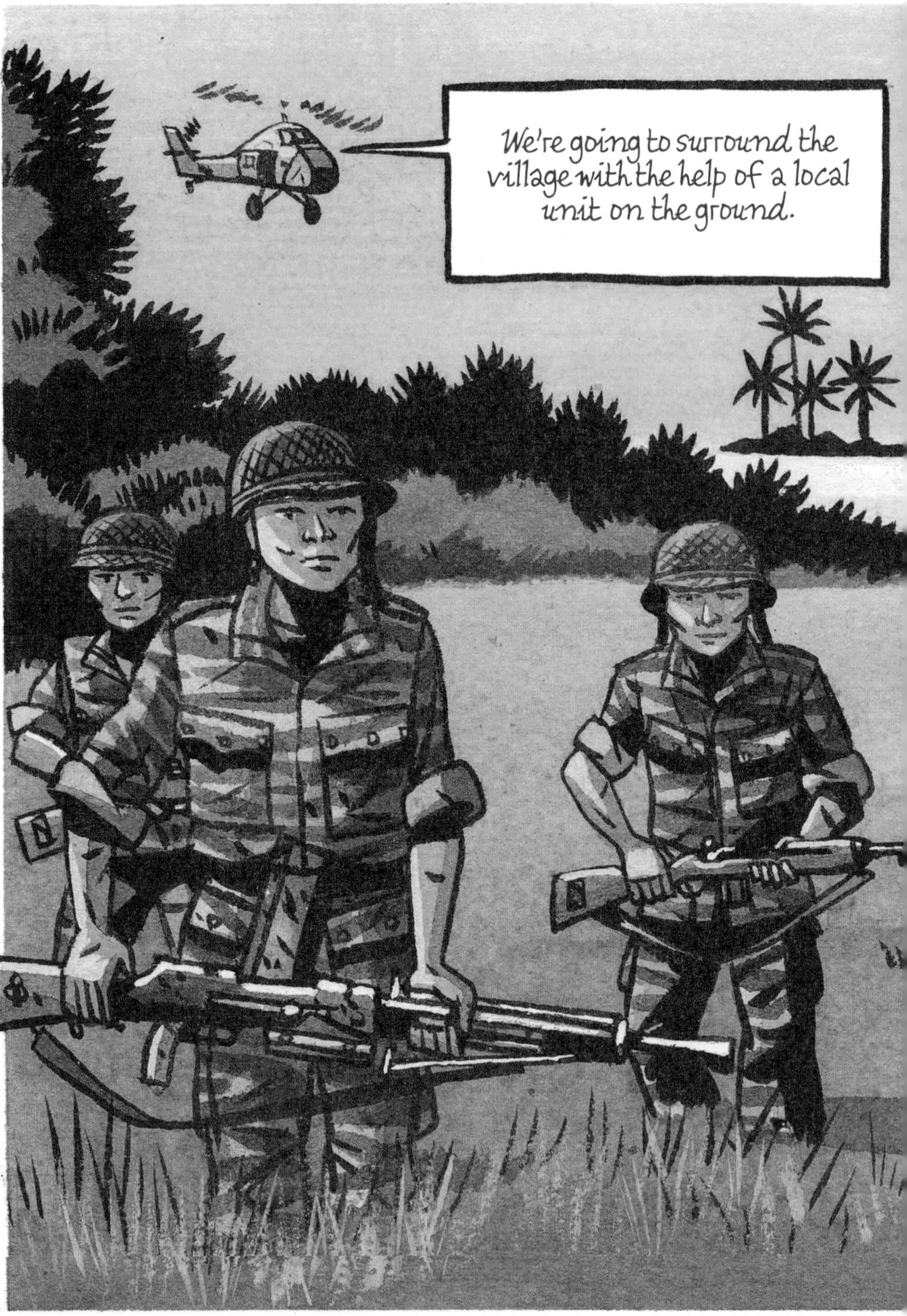
We're going to surround the village with the help of a local unit on the ground.

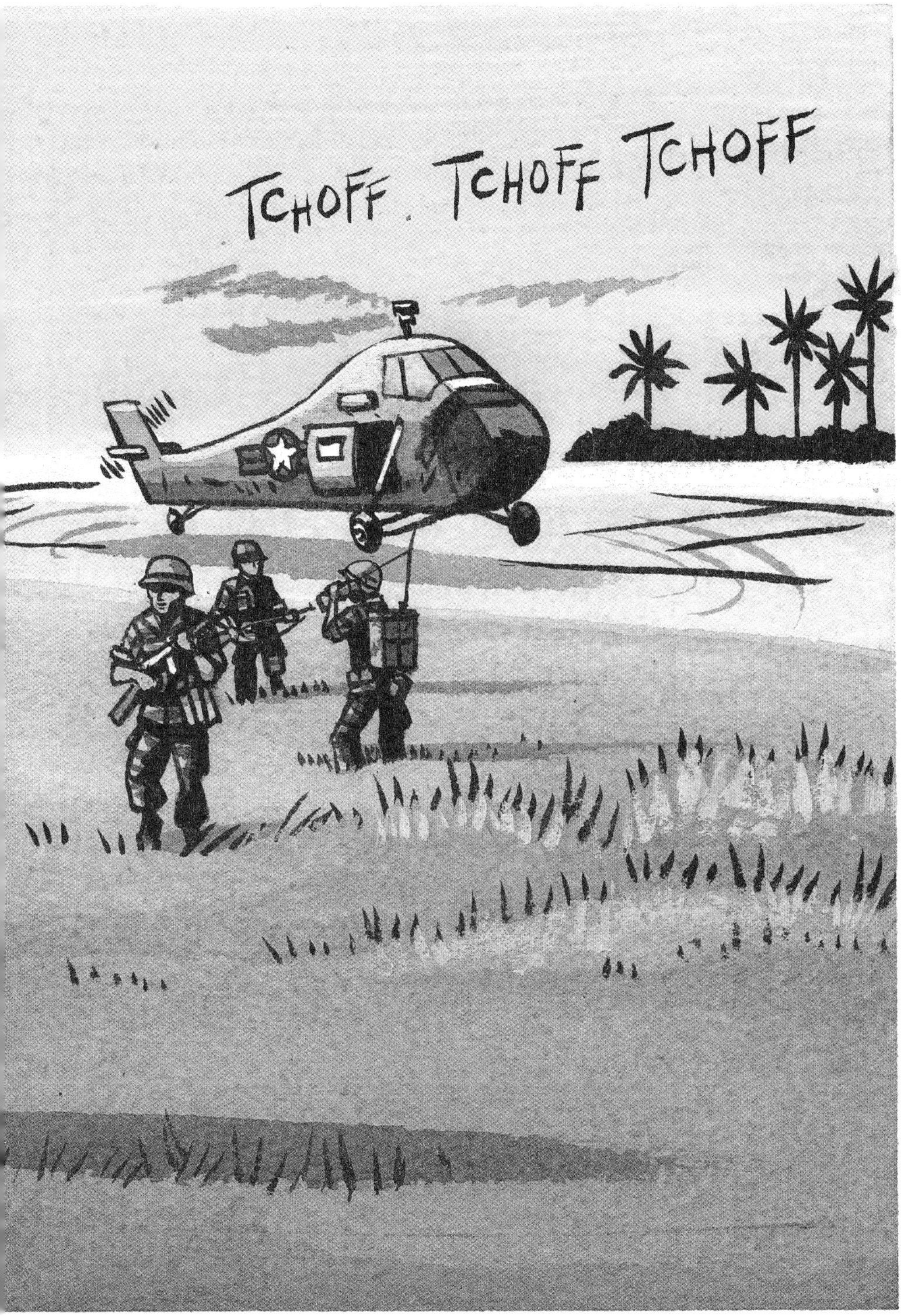
TCHOFF TCHOFF TCHOFF

Using the element of surprise, the soldiers cut off the village, a reputed Viêt-Cong hide-out. Their goal: obtain information and dismantle the network.

But the VC fought back only when they had the upper hand. Often they had been tipped off and the hunt was futile.

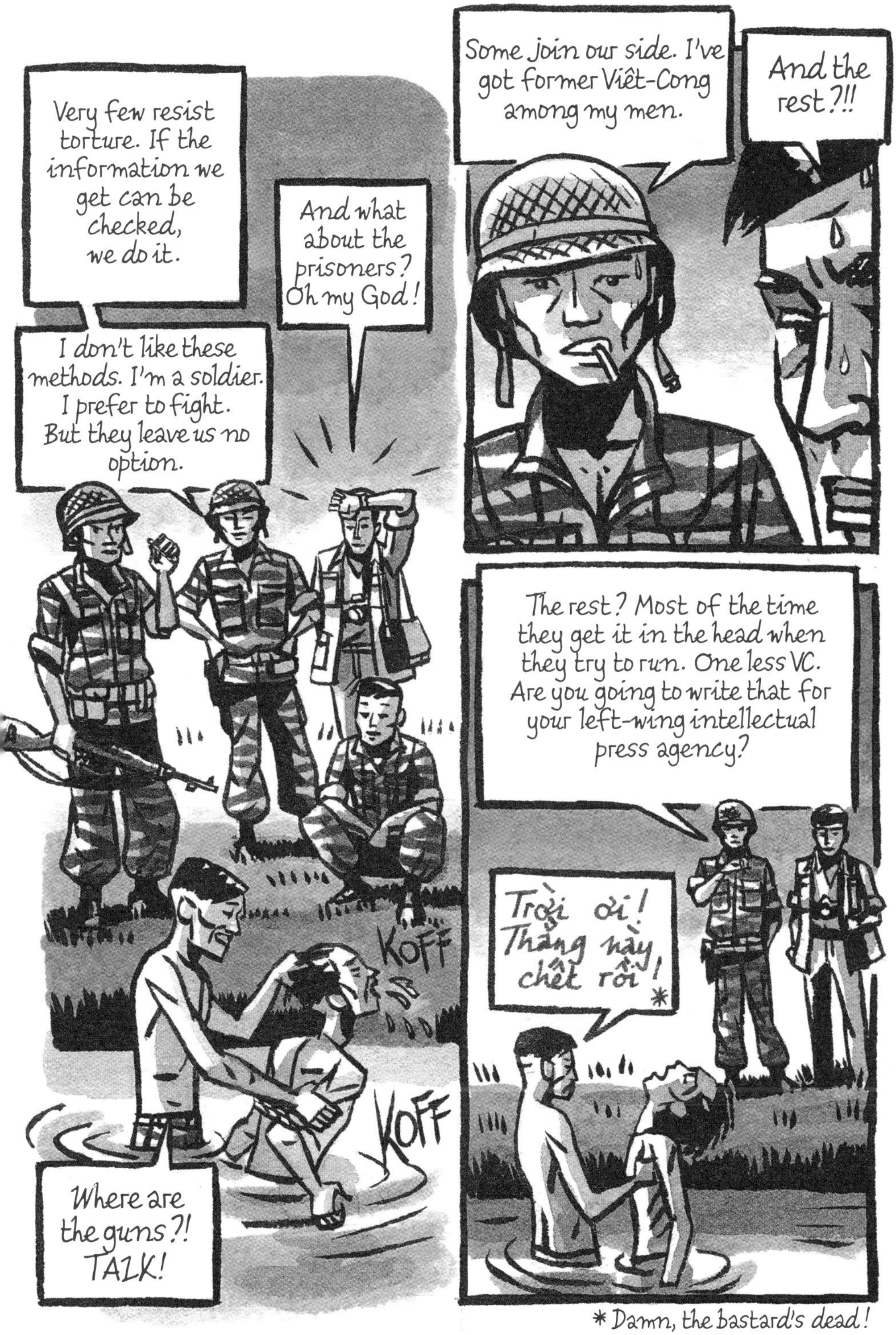
Very few resist torture. If the information we get can be checked, we do it.
I don't like these methods. I'm a soldier. I prefer to fight. But they leave us no option.
And what about the prisoners? Oh my God!
KOFF
KOFF
Where are the guns?! TALK!
Some join our side. I've got former Viêt-Cong among my men.
And the rest?!!
The rest? Most of the time they get it in the head when they try to run. One less VC. Are you going to write that for your left-wing intellectual press agency?
Trời ơi! Thằng nầy chết rồi!*

* Damn, the bastard's dead!

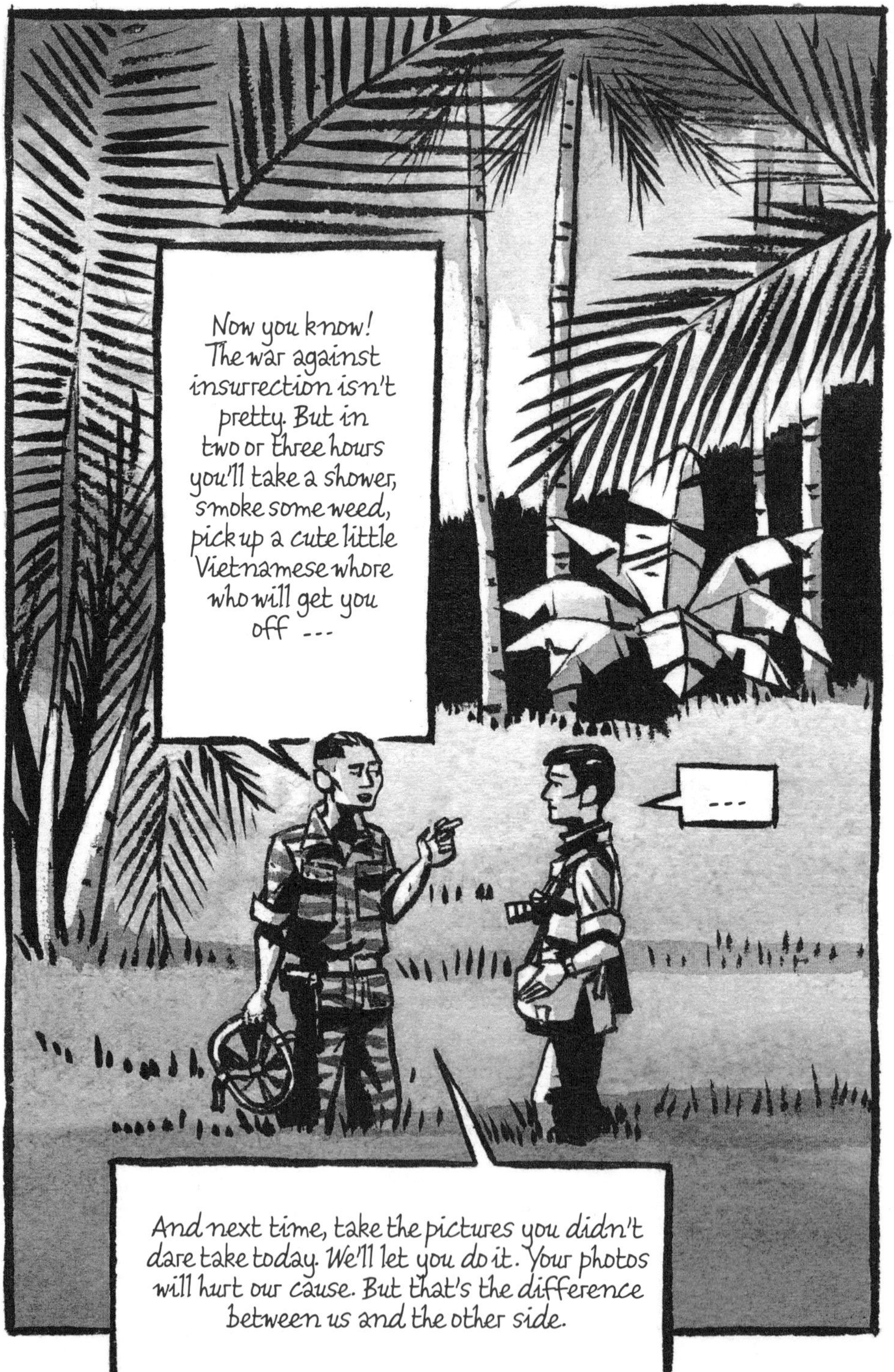
Now you know! The war against insurrection isn't pretty. But in two or three hours you'll take a shower, smoke some weed, pick up a cute little Vietnamese whore who will get you off ---
---
And next time, take the pictures you didn't dare take today. We'll let you do it. Your photos will hurt our cause. But that's the difference between us and the other side.

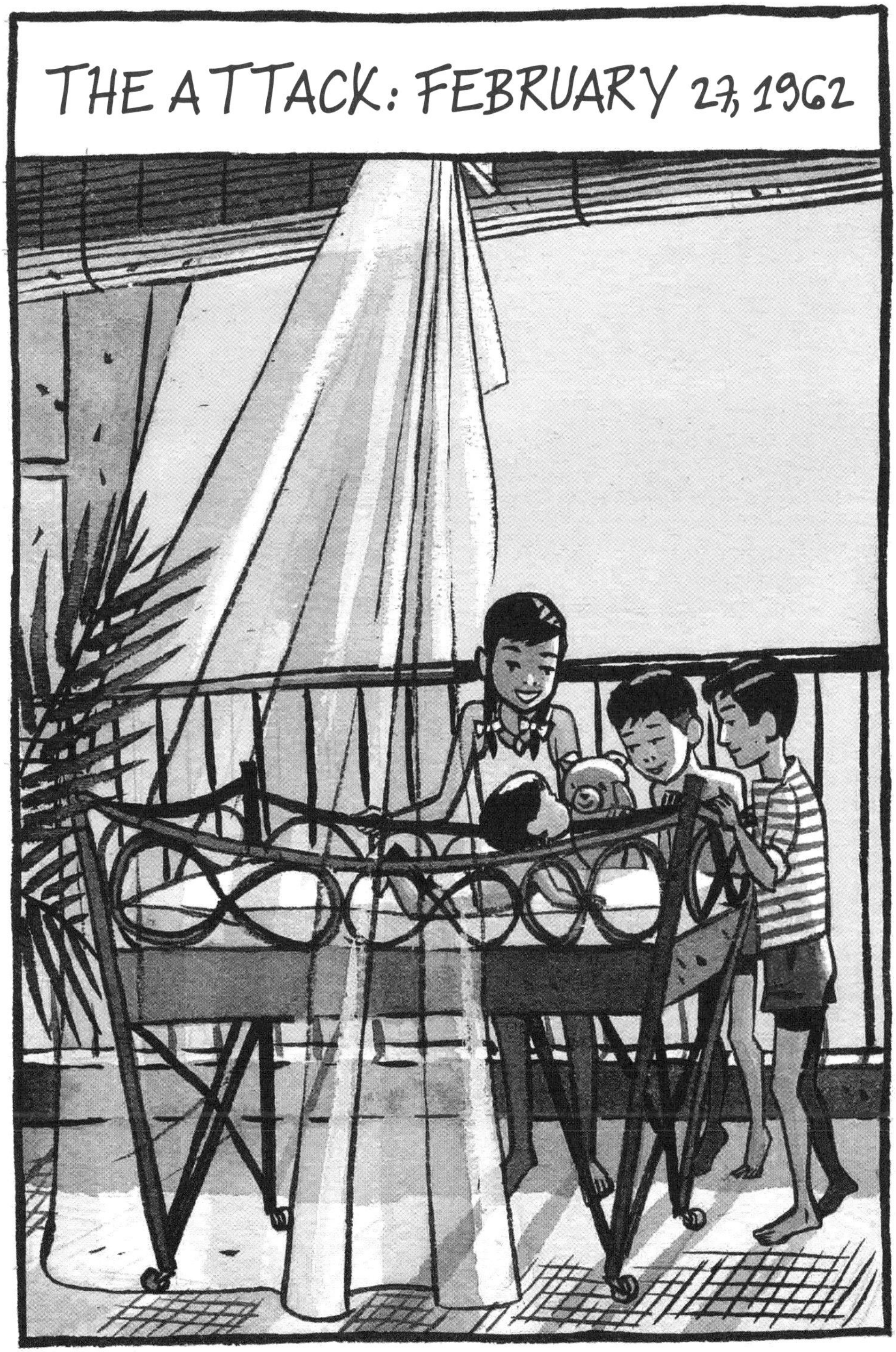
THE ATTACK: FEBRUARY 27, 1962

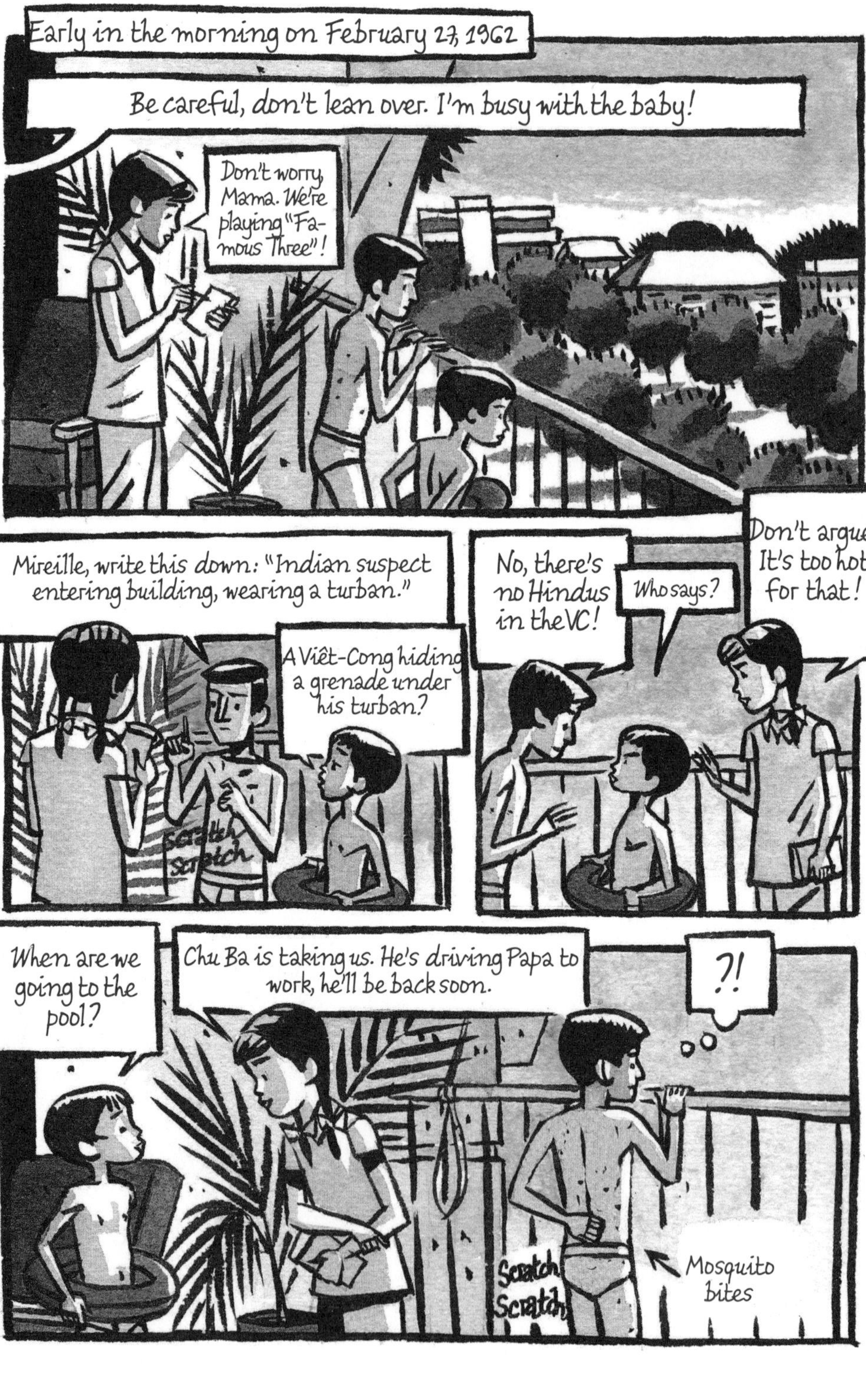
Early in the morning on February 27, 1962
Be careful, don't lean over. I'm busy with the baby!
Don't worry, Mama. We're playing "Famous Three"!
Mireille, write this down: "Indian suspect entering building, wearing a turban."
A Viêt-Cong hiding a grenade under his turban?
Scratch Scratch
No, there's no Hindus in the VC!
Who says?
Don't argue. It's too hot for that!
When are we going to the pool?
Chu Ba is taking us. He's driving Papa to work, he'll be back soon.
?!
Scratch Scratch
Mosquito bites

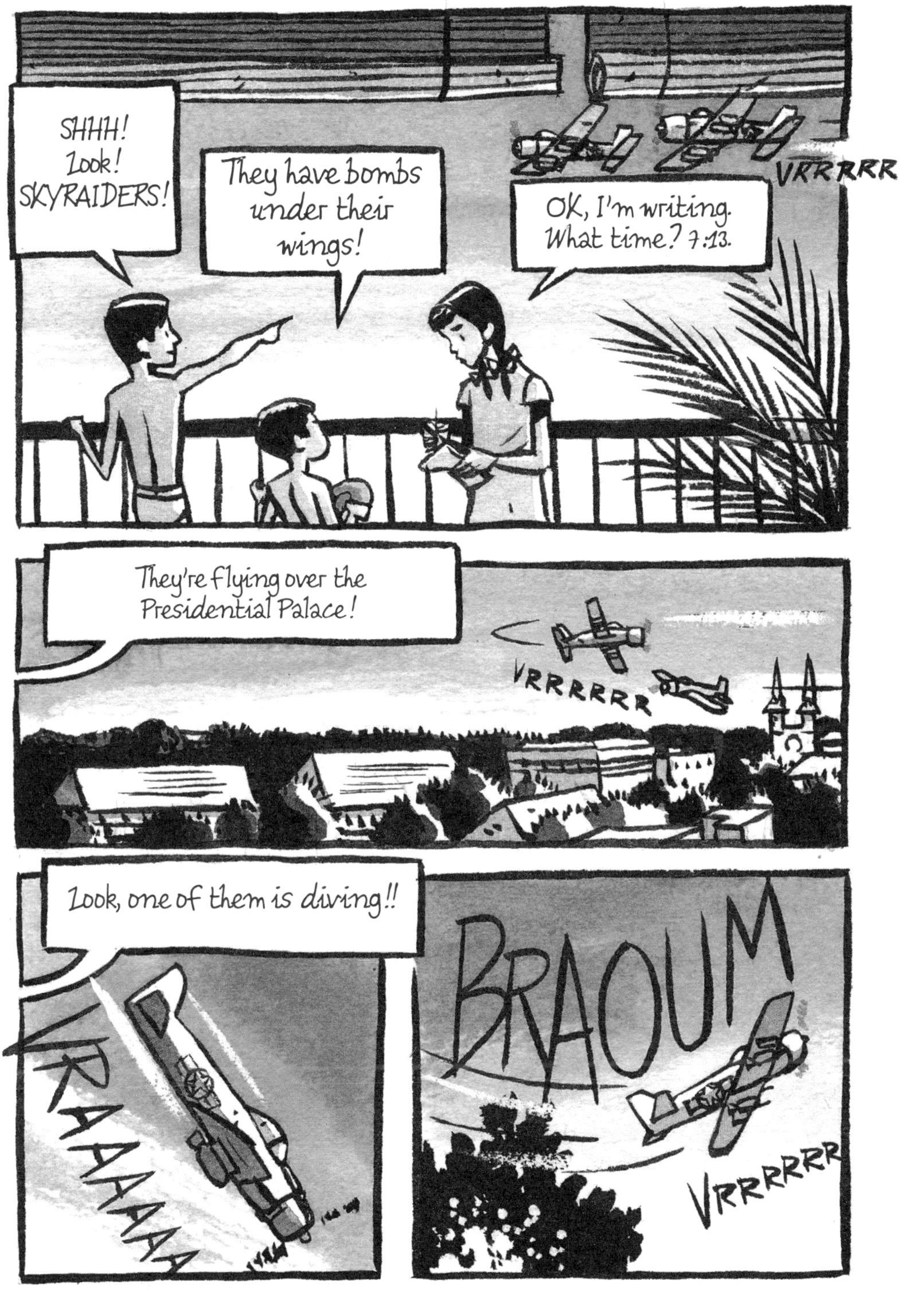
SHHH! Look! SKYRAIDERS!
They have bombs under their wings!
OK, I'm writing. What time? 7:13.
VRRRRRR
They're flying over the Presidential Palace!
VRRRRRRR
Look, one of them is diving!!
VRAAAAAA
BRAOUM
VRRRRRR

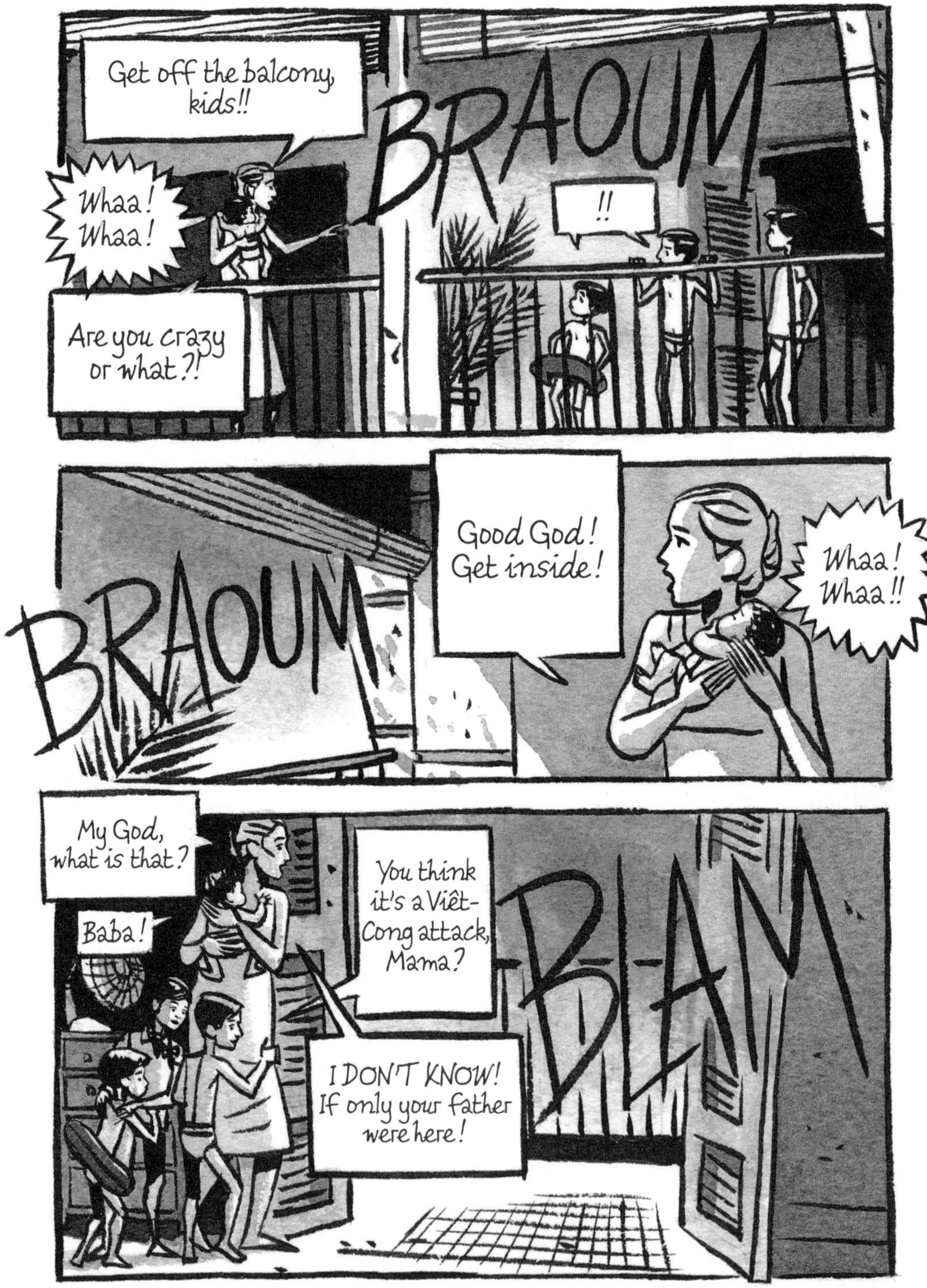
Get off the balcony, kids!!
Whaa! Whaa!
Are you crazy or what?!
BRAOUM
!!
BRAOUM
Good God! Get inside!
Whaa! Whaa!!
My God, what is that?
Baba!
You think it's a Viêt-Cong attack, Mama?
I DON'T KNOW! If only your father were here!
BLAM

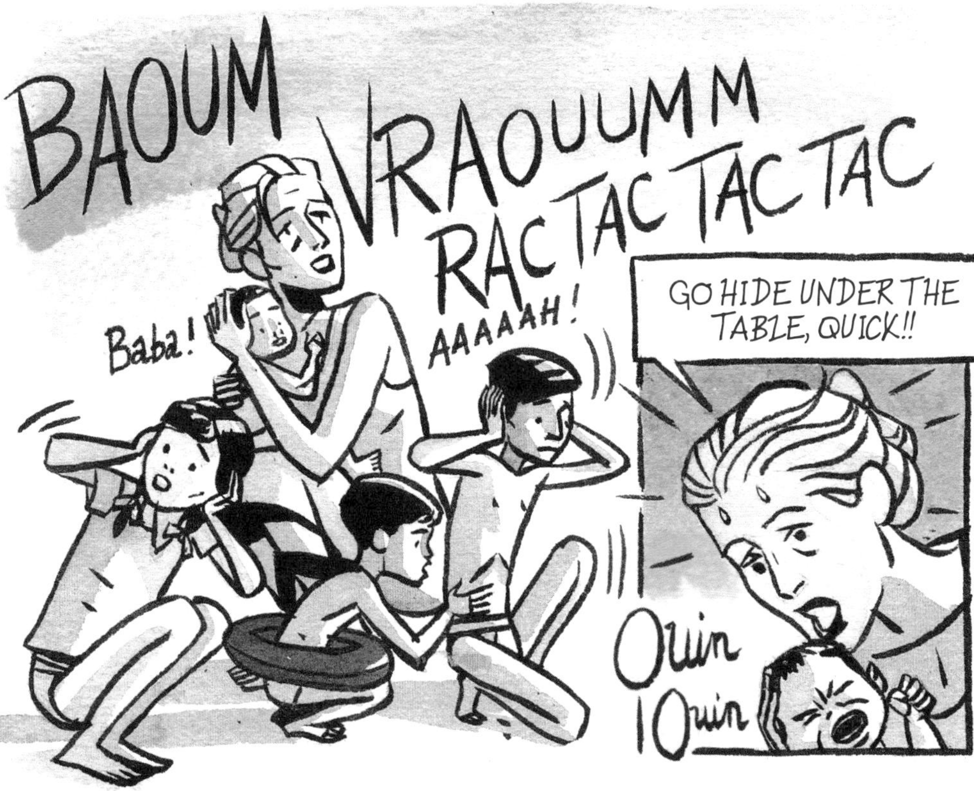
BAOUM
VRAOUUMM
RACTACTACTAC
Baba!
AAAAAH!
GO HIDE UNDER THE TABLE, QUICK!!
Ouin
Ouin

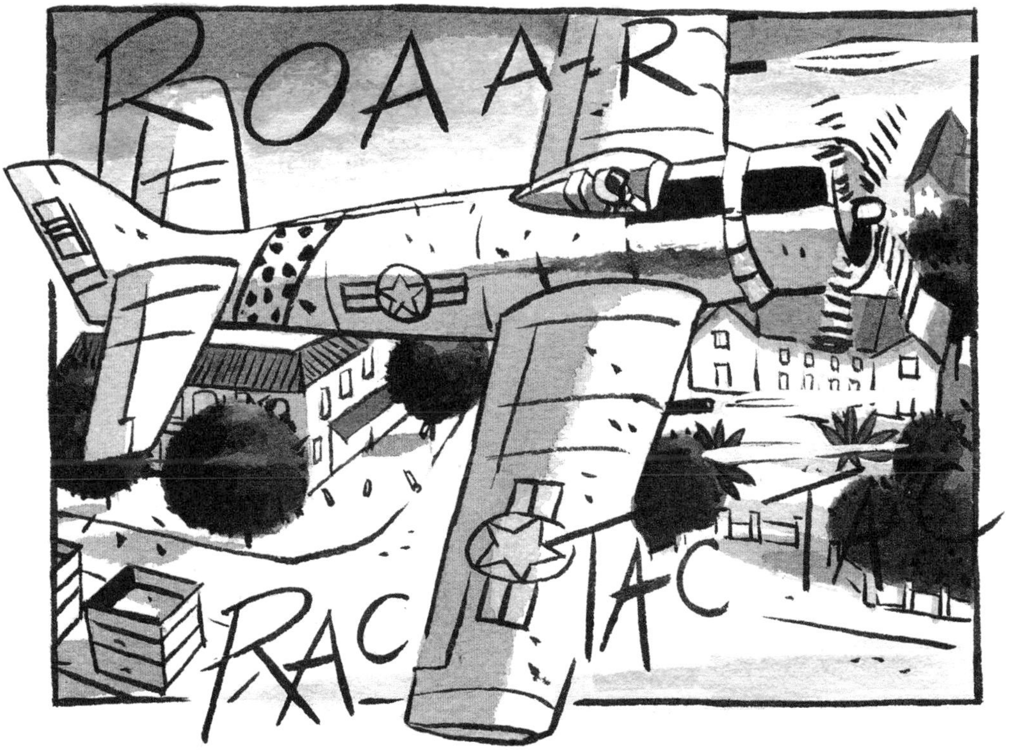
ROAAR
RAC TAC

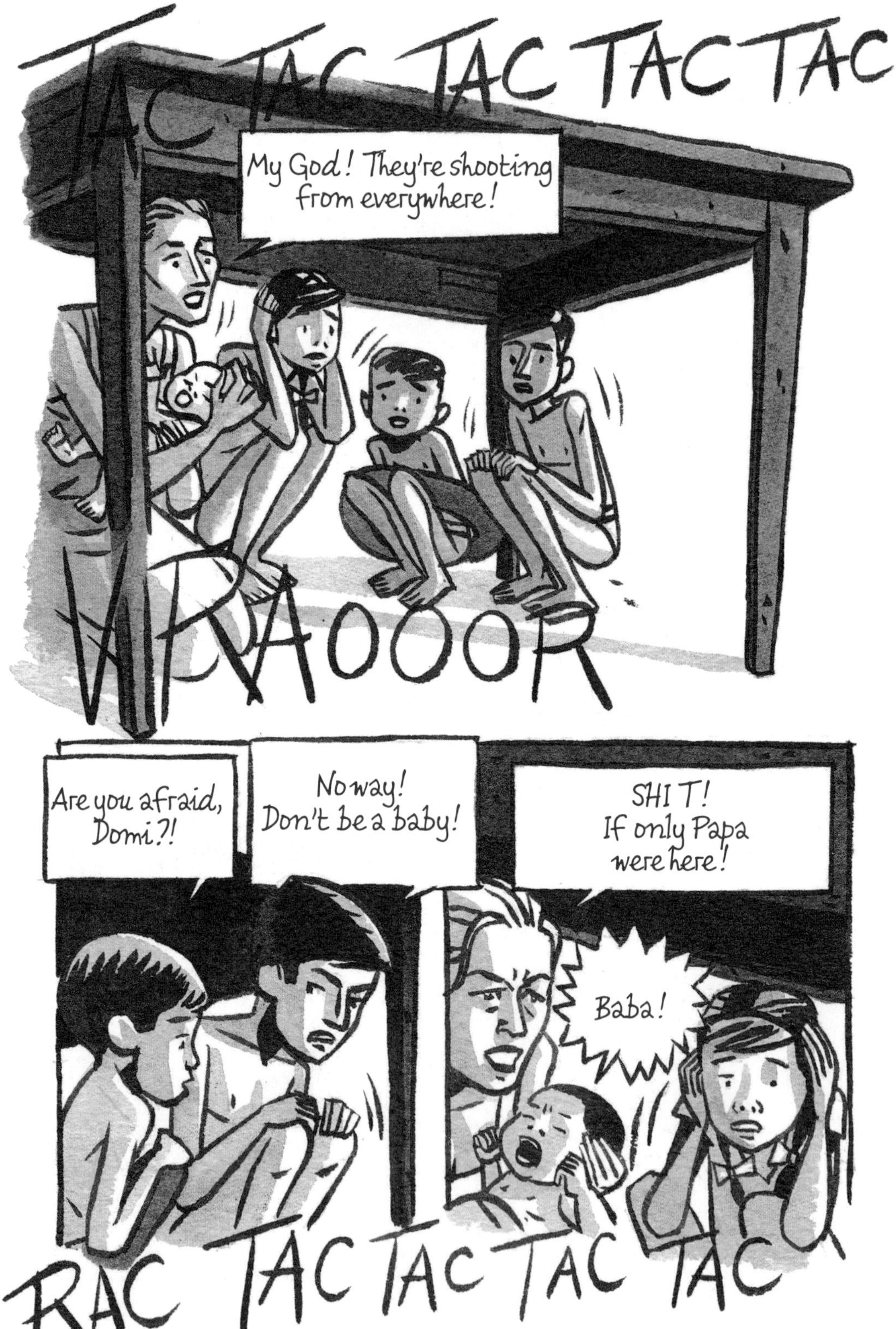
TAC TAC TAC TAC TAC
My God! They're shooting from everywhere!
VRAOOOR
Are you afraid, Domi?!
No way! Don't be a baby!
SHIT! If only Papa were here!
Baba!
RAC TAC TAC TAC TAC

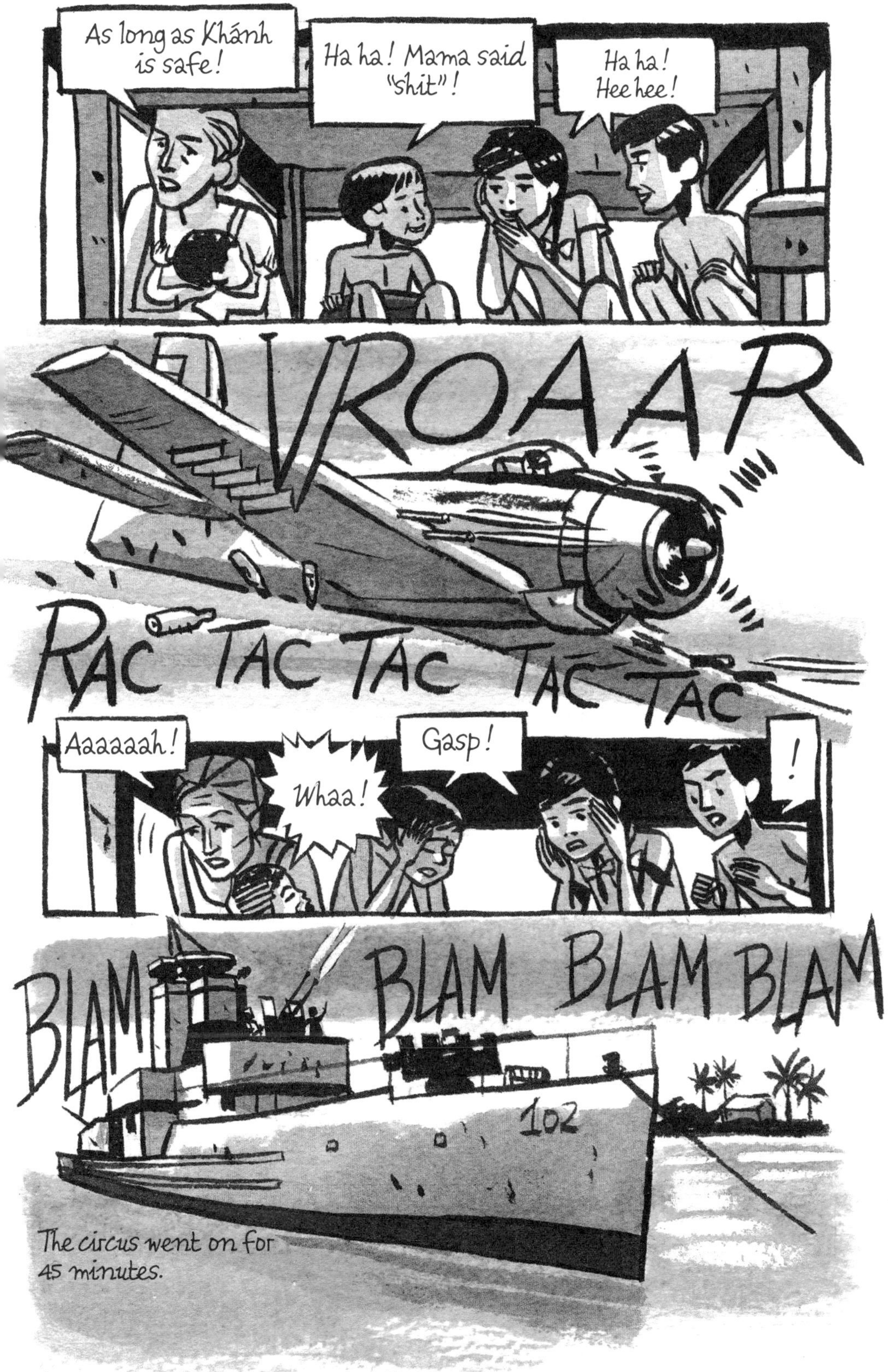
As long as Khánh is safe!
Ha ha! Mama said "shit"!
Ha ha! Hee hee!
VROAAR
RAC TAC TAC TAC TAC
Aaaaaah!
Whaa!
Gasp!
!
BLAM BLAM BLAM BLAM
102
The circus went on for 45 minutes.

The explosions grew less frequent, then we heard tank tracks on the asphalt, and once more, horns, bicycle bells, and voices. Life was returning.

Our phone rang.

Oh, finally, Khánh! I was worried sick!

Baba!

Baba!

Are you and the children all right?!

Yes. But we were terrified! I thought it was a Viêt-Cong attack!

No, it was an attempt on President Diêm's life. I'll be right there!

That evening, our parents talked about the event.

One of the Skyraiders was shot down over the Saigon River and the pilot was recovered. They must have tortured him to find out how widespread the plot was. The other pilot was able to land in Cambodia.

Baba!

Good Lord, we have a president who can't command the respect of his army!

TAC TAC TAC TAC!

In any case, the whole thing turned my insides upside down!

How do you think they tortured the pilot?

I heard they use electricity ...

The next day, with Chu Ba, we joined the flock of curious people who came to see the damage done to the Independence Palace. The comments flew thick and fast.

It was a surgical strike!

Come this way, you'll see better!

C'rem... C'rem... Cà rem!*

Chú Ba Domi Marco

One of the wings of the former palace of the Governor General of Indochina was destroyed.

The pilots were aiming for the president and his brother Ngô Dinh Nhu.

And Madame Nhu too!

CLIC CLAC

Just one problem: they got the wrong wing! The president and the Nhu family live in the undamaged part.

Có thể ăn rem, cà rem, Chú Ba?*

* Ice cream!

* Can we have an ice cream, Chu Ba?

108

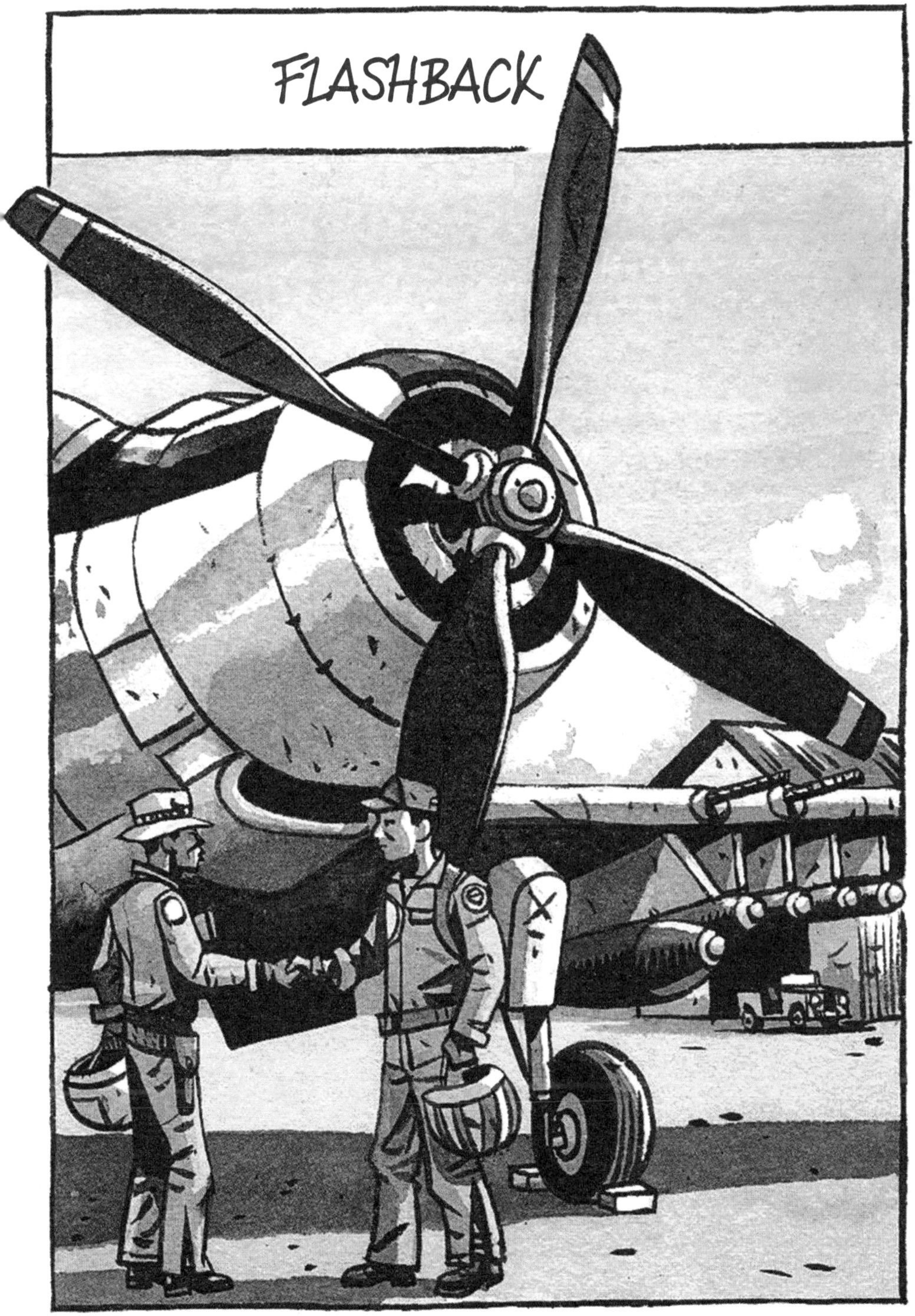
FLASHBACK

Fifty years later, I was able to put together the facts behind the spectacular attack in February 1962.

VRRRRRRRRR

At dawn on February 27, 1962, two Skyraiders took off from the Biên Hoa base for a ground support mission in the delta.

But instead, the pilots headed for downtown Saigon.

The one who lives in a palace? Affirmative!

I think I'll go say hi to my old aunt!

The Douglas Skyraider was a robust, propeller-driven fighter-bomber, and very efficient when it came to surgical strikes like dumping napalm. Among other nicknames, it was called the "Crazy Water Buffalo."

When the first bombs fell, President Diêm was reading a biography of George Washington, a gift from an American diplomat.

With the first explosion, an aid burst into President Diêm's bedroom.

Mr. President, we must take shelter!

After recovering from the shock, the Presidential Guard fired back.

Aerial reinforcements were called in.

Two Skyraiders from the First Squadron— shoot them down! Blast them out of the sky!

The warships tied up in the Saigon River joined the engagement.

The duel was on between the renegade Skyraiders and the fighters sent to shoot them down.

Lt. Quốc's plane was hit by the ship's anti-aircraft fire.

The plane crashed into the Saigon River. The pilot managed to eject and was pulled out along with his plane.

Lt. Quôc was immediately interrogated to find out how widespread the plot was.

Sometime later ---

Cu and I did it on our own ---

The military—the real ones, not the careerists—want to win this war ---

The president is too soft! He's a civilian!

And his advisors are lousy!

I think he's telling the truth.

That's the fourth attack on our president. We think the Americans are behind it. Keep going!

Aaaah!

SCHLAAK

TALK!

Uhuuh!

SCHTAAKK

THAT'S ENOUGH! TAKE HIM TO THE LOCK-UP!

The Head of Military Security knew the pilots' families. Everyone knew each other in Saigon. Complex family relations were the key to Vietnamese society. After the attack, Lt. Quốc was imprisoned. In 1963 he was freed, after the coup d'état that ended Diêm's regime. He died in 1965 during a bombing mission in the North.

The pilot of the second Skyraider managed to shake off his adversaries by making a crash landing in Phnom Penh, Cambodia. His plane had been hit 50 times.

Lt. Cu was sure he had eliminated President Diêm and his entourage. He issued a statement to the journalists who had rushed to the airstrip.

The Vietnamese people and elements of the army detest the regime imposed by Ngô Dinh Diêm and his family!

Cambodia gave political asylum to the renegade pilot. Lt. Cu lived in exile there until the November 1963 coup d'état that toppled the Diêm regime. As of 2016, he was still alive, dividing his time between Vietnam and the United States.

What really happened inside the Presidential Palace? In the shelter, President Diêm was joined by his brother and advisor, Nhu, accompanied by his four children.

Thuc, the archbishop of Huê and the elder brother of the Ngô clan, had been praying since dawn in the palace chapel. The bombs spared him too. Divine intervention, in his opinion.

SANTA MARIA!

BRAOUM

Madame Nhu was the last to arrive, safe despite falling through a floor split open by a bomb. She came through with just a few scratches.

Heaven be praised, children!

You're safe and sound!

!

Má!

Má!

The only victims of the attack were three palace domestics. Around 8 o'clock that same day, the president gave a short speech on the radio.

Thanks to the protection of the Almighty, I will continue my mandate and conduct our nation's affairs ---

After which, Diêm took a helicopter to inspect an outpost in a distant province.
As a precaution, all Air Force flights were suspended ---

Two days later, United States Ambassador Nolting paid a visit to Diêm at the Gia Long Palace, since Independence Palace was unusable.

Mr. President, do you think this attack---

--- is simply the work of two officers gone astray?

Yes. I met the pilots of the 1st Fighter Squadron at the Biên Hoa base---

They are young --- immature and impetuous, you know, but they sincerely regret what their two hot-head comrades did! I believe they are loyal.

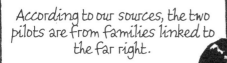

According to our sources, the two pilots are from families linked to the far right.

Those people think I'm not hard enough on the Communists, and that they'd do better!

The two plotters were no doubt influenced by the negative image of me in the foreign press.

Your press is sabotaging our efforts! The Communist government in Hanoi has free rein!

Yes, but that's what makes you different. Freedom of the press is at the heart of our American idea of democracy. Mr. President, you have our complete support!

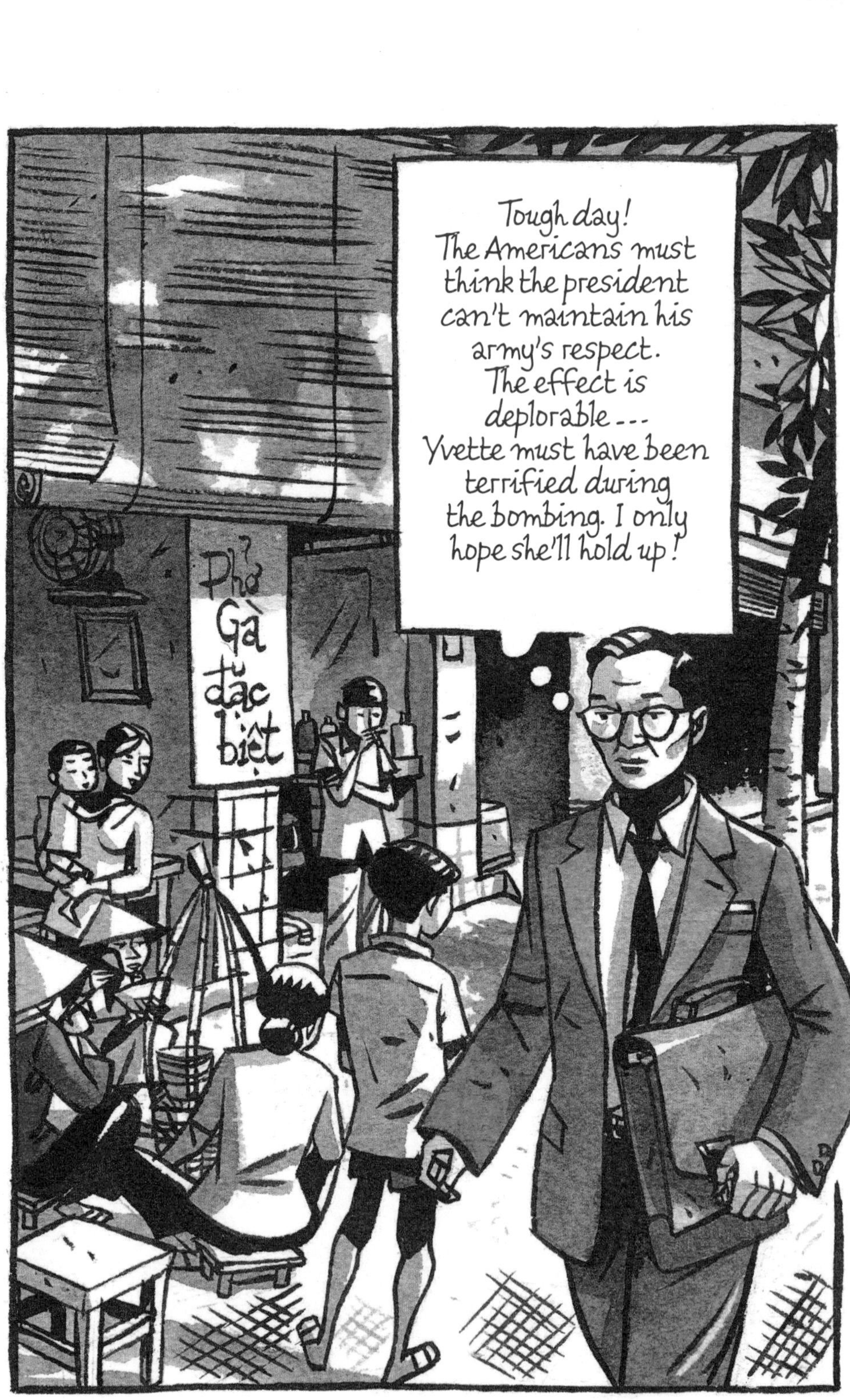
Tough day! The Americans must think the president can't maintain his army's respect. The effect is deplorable... Yvette must have been terrified during the bombing. I only hope she'll hold up!
Phở Gà đặc biệt

MADAME

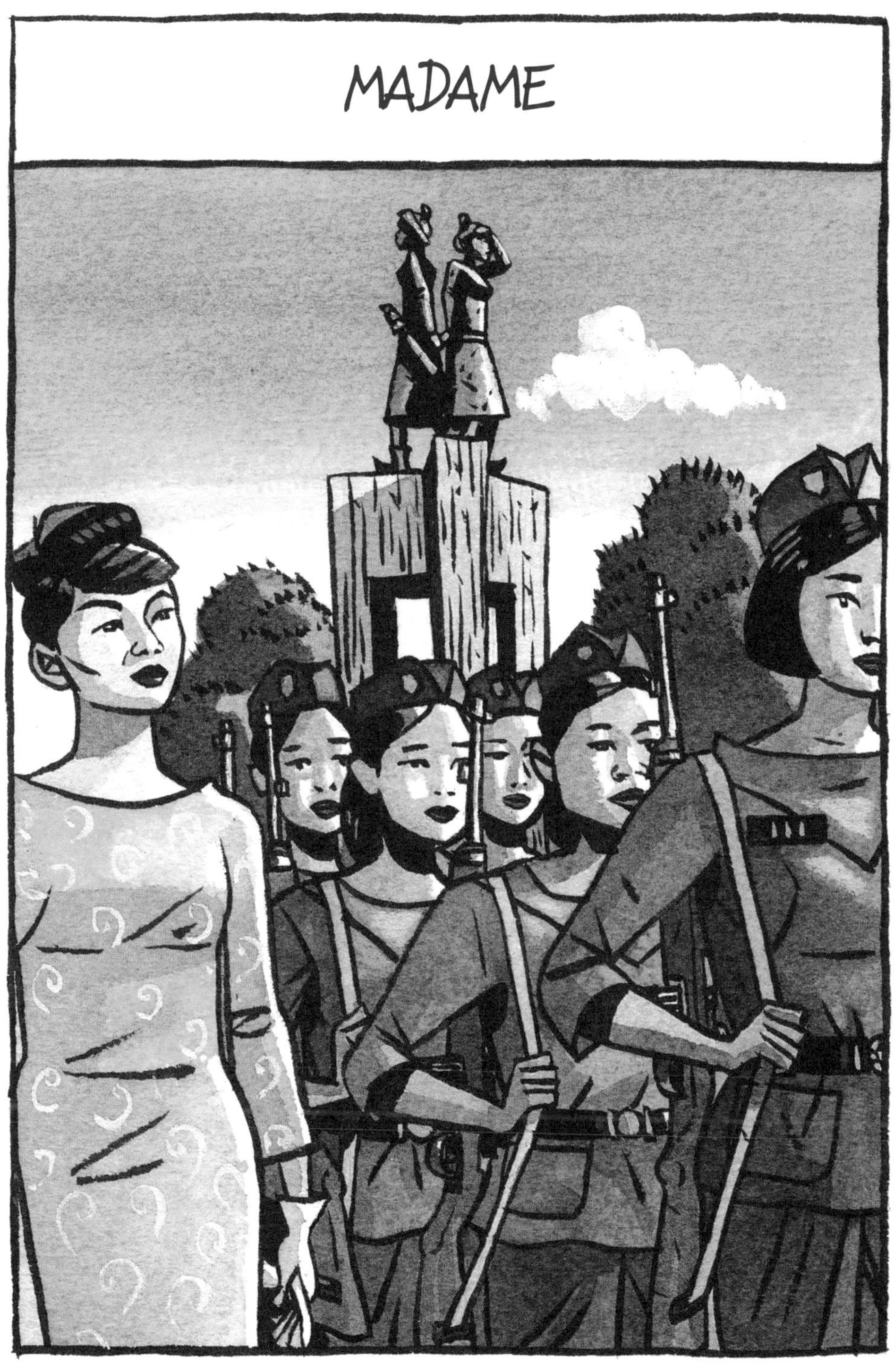

In 1962, a most unusual parade took place on the day dedicated to the two Trung sisters, first-century heroines who repelled the Chinese invaders at the head of an army of women.

Look, Domi, there are women soldiers in the parade!

After the traditional floats, a women's battalion paraded in arms. They were Madame Nhu's "Jeunes Républicaines," the Sisters of the Republic, the armed branch of her feminist organization, the Women's Solidarity Movement: the WSM. Madame Nhu herself designed the "Star Trek"-like uniforms. *

Look, they've got American M1 carbines!

I wouldn't know. I'm looking at their titties!

* Episode 45 of "Star Trek," entitled 'A Private Little War' (February 1968), was directly inspired by the beginnings of American involvement in Vietnam: Madame Nhu, the Viêt-Cong, the Green Berets, etc.

124

Mama's letter to her parents in Saint-Malo, March 1962:

The population was entertained by the parade of the Trung sisters with the battalions of women soldiers, very smartly dressed, by the way. That's Madame Nhu's idea, and it's pretty clever, since if women got involved with defending the country, the way they did long ago against the Chinese, things would look dim for the enemy. But the men just laugh, cowardly as usual. They're the ones most afraid, and afraid too of losing face. Which could be the reason behind the bombing of the Presidential Palace.

The two February 27 pilots with wounded male pride, deciding to kill Madame Nhu? They were aiming for the whole presidential clan, the Ngô family.

Madame Nhu saw herself as a modern, emancipated Vietnamese woman, and in a country where women were expected to display submissive behavior, some people were irritated by her.
She restyled the traditional Vietnamese dress, giving it a more open neck, less stiff than the usual Chinese collar. She also designed the parade uniforms for the Sisters of the Republic, whom she called her "darlings."

Traditional dress moder-
nized by Madame Nhu

Lê-Thuy, her daughter,
in the Sisters uniform

For her militia, Madame* modeled herself on her enemy. Among the Communists and in the NLF, women were fighters too. They played a considerable role during the wars in Vietnam. Yet once victory was secured, they went back to their traditional roles.

Oh, what a kick!

BLAM

Colt 45

Smith & Wesson 38 Special

US Winchester M1 carbine

People said that the "Jeunes Républicaines" included former prostitutes, since Madame led a crusade against vice. With the influx of American advisors—12,000 in 1962—and their dollars, all sorts of contraband became available. Madame ordered the nightclubs and dancehalls closed. Western dances (like the twist, the cha-cha, and slow ones) were banned.

* Back then, if you said "Madame," everyone knew you meant Madame Nhu.

The woman the American press called "the Dragon Lady" (an allusion to the Machiavellian Asian heroine of the Milton Caniff comics) preached moral order and virtue as panaceas in the fight to the finish against the Viêt-Cong, who were puritan and spartan.

* Dances were very risqué for the Vietnamese.

As a member of the National Assembly, Madame Nhu voted in laws forbidding divorce, adultery (quite the ambition!), polygamy (!) and abortion. These measures were meant to protect Vietnamese women. But no law could protect Madame Nhu against her own insatiable lust for power.

When it came to the men of the Saigon regime, Mama often questioned their virility and willingness to fight. When you're afraid, big muscles are reassuring. The Vietnamese are smaller than Westerners, but appearances can be deceiving.

That reception was very entertaining!

Yes --- But your colleagues are rather effeminate. We won't beat the Viêt-Cong with that!

Marco, why aren't you sleeping?

Mama, tomorrow can we buy a sword at the Botanical Gardens?

ZIIIIP

It was true: the leaders of the Communist North were beaten into shape by their war against the French, whereas our elite, in the South, grew up in the lap of the former colonial power and were more skilled with the pen than the gun—at ease in the city, not in the field.

Papa was devoted to his work and in his way he contributed to the war effort. He was at home very seldom. As Mama said, "Your father works like a nigger." That's the way people talked at the time.

All right, to bed! It's late. I start at six tomorrow!

The young Republic of Vietnam assumed the mantle of the former colonial power and even adopted its trappings, including the famous white tussah suit described by writer Marguerite Duras as the emblem of white domination in Asia. The suit immediately placed us on the side of the bourgeois West at a time when camouflage (Castro, Guevara, Nasser), Chinese pajamas (Mao, Hô Chi Minh), and the languti (Gandhi) were in fashion.

Our father's job provided a black Peugeot for official use.

His day began at the Presidential Palace, since he was also the president's official interpreter. Statesmen, generals, journalists, and the clergy all came to take the pulse of the regime and offer advice. Diêm understood English, but he preferred that his statements be faithfully translated. I questioned my father about those days.

Often Papa came home from the office exhausted with a troubled, weary expression. Too beat to play with us ---

But as soon as he took off his civil servant suit, he relaxed and forgot his troubles.

Often there was tension at the house. From time to time, Mother turned into a despot, and her tyranny took the form of a maniacal need for cleanliness and order. She declared war on "filth."

In these "clean sweep" phases, she seemed immune to fatigue and filled with a strange feeling of superiority..

Often these outbursts happened on weekends or during vacation. We were a burden on Mama during these periods of forced togetherness.

We were her hostages: helpless spectators, subject to her attacks. Even Papa came in for his share of blame.

Mireille's letter to our grandparents in Saint-Malo, April 1961: "A few days ago we went to see 'Constantine and the Cross.'* On Easter we cleaned the kitchen. I learned to swim and I have lots of fun at the pool ---"

* A grandiose historical film by Lionello De Felice, from 1960, in Totalscope.

What we really *didn't* understand, since it wasn't official, was that Mama suffered from manic depression, which today we call bipolar: a disorder in which the victim experiences highs and lows, like a series of strong tides.

Low   Ebb   Slack   Flood

When she was feeling low, the slightest effort was beyond her capacities ---

I can't go on!

--- which was followed by periods of hyperactivity, sometimes euphoric, other times aggressive. Nothing can predict the mood of someone who has this disorder.

MAR-VEL-OUS!

GET TO WORK!

In the most extreme cases, the bipolar person seems to be possessed by a sort of demon. Dr. Jekyll turns into Mr. Hyde. The person isn't always aware of her state. The disorder is genetic, but can also be caused by shock, loss, or fear.

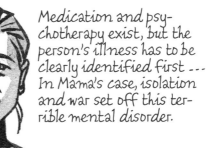

Medication and psychotherapy exist, but the person's illness has to be clearly identified first --- In Mama's case, isolation and war set off this terrible mental disorder.

It wasn't easy holding back Mama's tidal waves, and her sense of being sick of everything. She swung from *dejection* to *vituperation*. Fatigue or emotion could send her spiraling toward one or the other.

The Vietnamese were acclimatized to war. They had to be. And often they were in denial.

THE CATHOLICS OF VIETNAM

At Easter,* we were given an illustrated edition of the Bible, "La Bible en images" (published by Desclée de Brouwer, 1951). It became my bedside reading along with the picture book encyclopedia called "Tout l'univers," purchased every week at the Portail bookstore in Eden Passage, famously described by Marguerite Duras in "Eden Cinéma."

I was like a fish in water in the oriental universe of the Old Testament. All those nations, dominating and self-assured, massacring each other? I knew about that!

The law is a voice of terrible words, and was given amidst a tempest of wind, thunder, and lightning, attended with an earthquake. After all, it was more like whispering than roaring.

* As I was writing these lines on April 25, 2011, Easter Day, my father told me that Madame Nhu had died at age 87 in a clinic in Rome.

In 1962, the voice of Vietnamese Catholics was anything but a gentle whispering. It shouted its anti-Communist feelings to the sky. President Diêm depended on the Catholics, a dynamic minority reinforced by the influx of the faithful from the North, fleeing the Marxist regime; they were not inclined to indulge Hanoi's dogma.

We had to sell our property on the sidewalk for nothing ---

--- before stealing away like thieves in the night. It wasn't easy to start from scratch in the South

NEVER AGAIN!

Through hard work, Catholic refugees from the North acquired top positions in a country led by a president who shared their faith. Soon rumors flew, accusing him of religious favoritism.

If I were Catholic, by now I'd be head of a province!

And I'd be a colonel!!

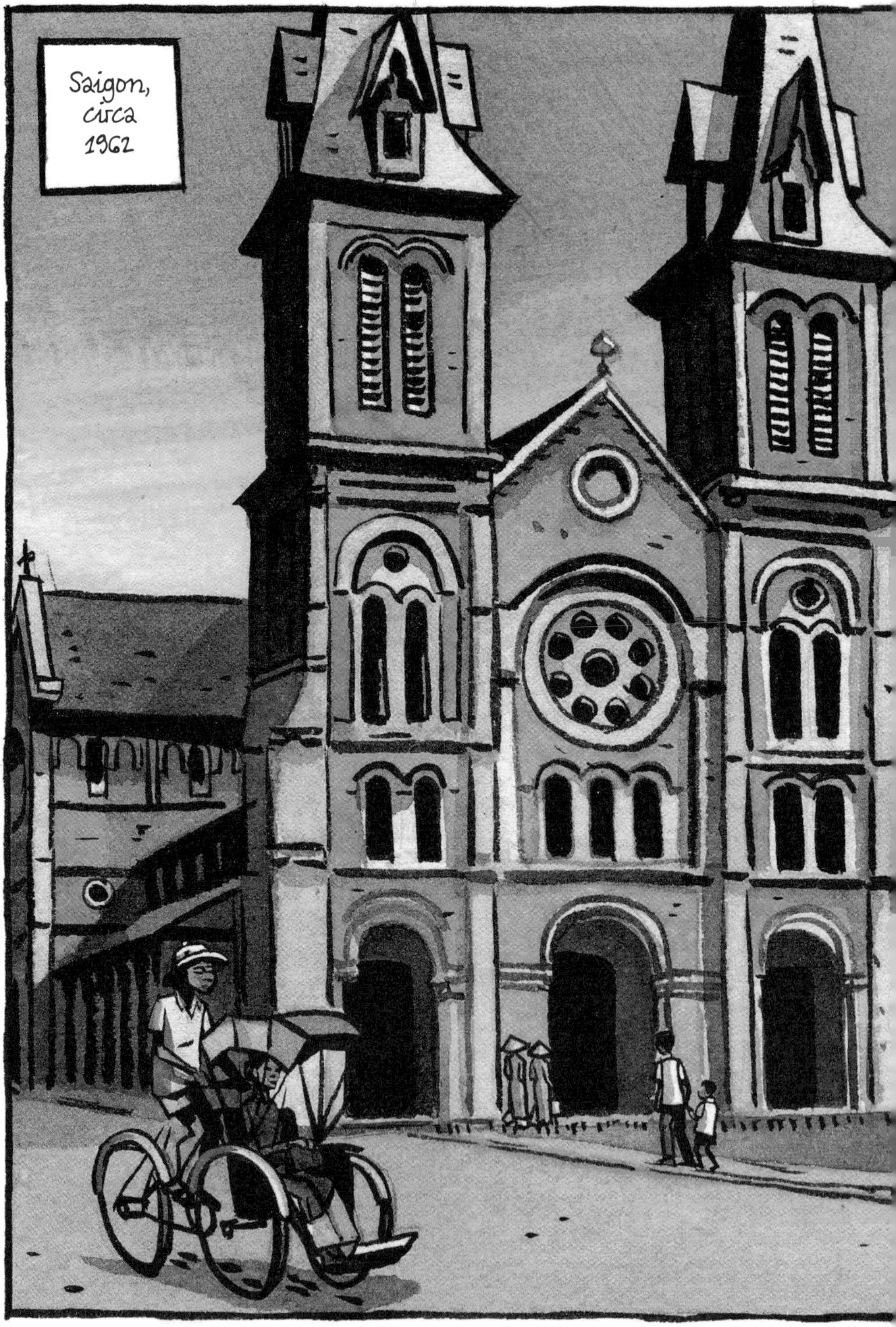
Saigon,
circa
1962

Vietnamese Catholics seemed to have things going their way. In 1960, John F. Kennedy—America's first Catholic president—gave Diêm the support of the most powerful Western nation. To thank him for his help in his anti-Marxist crusade, Diêm renamed the square in front of Notre Dame de Saigon cathedral after Kennedy.

Before becoming JFK Square, this piece of land was named for a French missionary from the time of Louis XVI, Monsignor Pigneau de Béhaine, who had also rushed to the aid of a Vietnamese monarch toppled from his throne by a populist peasant rebellion,* creating a precedent in the process. The prince who got his throne back became the Emperor Gia Long. Some patriots considered him a traitor, since he had opened the henhouse of the nation to the Western fox.

Saigon, circa 1900

The Bishop of Adran, Pigneau de Béhaine, next to Prince Nguyên Canh, displays the 1787 treaty binding France and Vietnam.

Come on, faster!

UNH! UNH!

Tap Tap Tap Tap

* The Tây Son Rebellion (1770-1802). The boulevard we lived on was named after its charismatic leader, Nguyên Huê.

Easy to understand why the Catholics were accused of being believers in a foreign religion that helped the "European barbarians" establish themselves in Vietnam. Add to that a long history* of persecution, making Vietnamese Catholicism a faith forged by the executioner's sword and washed in the blood of martyrs.

Fervent convictions made the Catholic community the avant-garde in the anti-Communist struggle. In Vietnam, Catholics and Reds shared a dogmatic sense of faith. Though Marxists outstripped their adversaries when it came to the propensity to martyrdom.

* Christian missionaries first arrived in Indochina in the 16th century.

143

Papa was a fervent Catholic. His beliefs included charity and a good heart. Mama followed him on a simpler path. Every Sunday was Mass—Roman-style, of course.

Dominus vobiscum!

Et cum spiritu tuo!

I'm bored!

The spirits are about to speak!

Hee hee hee!

One day, intrigued by the priest's routine as he celebrated the Eucharist, I asked my father about it.

Papa, why is the priest putting the gold cups in the safe over there?

Shhh!

That's the tabernacle. The priest puts the ciborium that holds the hosts and the chalice with the wine there. That's where the wine and the hosts turn into the Blood and Body of Christ.

So bored!

!?

I swallowed his explanations about the mystery of Transubstantiation. No problem. Everything was possible in Vietnam. *

After Mass ---

What? The priest drinks blood? Like the cannibals in "Robinson Crusoe"?

Sigh!

Guess what Jesus Christ's father's name is!

Uh--- Dunno--- God?

Hey, boys, wait for me! I'm looking at the books.

No! Mr. Christ!!! Hee hee hee!

Ha ha ha!

TIỆM SÁCH VĂN HÓA

* In Vietnam, people sometimes drink blood to seal a pact. Whose blood? No idea.

I remember one Sunday before Mass. Chi Hai was smoothing my hair with a comb dipped in lavender-scented Eau de Cologne. That kept the lice away.

* Stop fidgeting, you'll be late for Mass!

I took a chance and touched Chi Hai's breast.

* No, really!

* You little rascal!

Chi Hai was eighteen at most. She lived in a Saigon slum. One day she took my sister Mireille there.

* You'll meet my mother!   * Great! And your father?

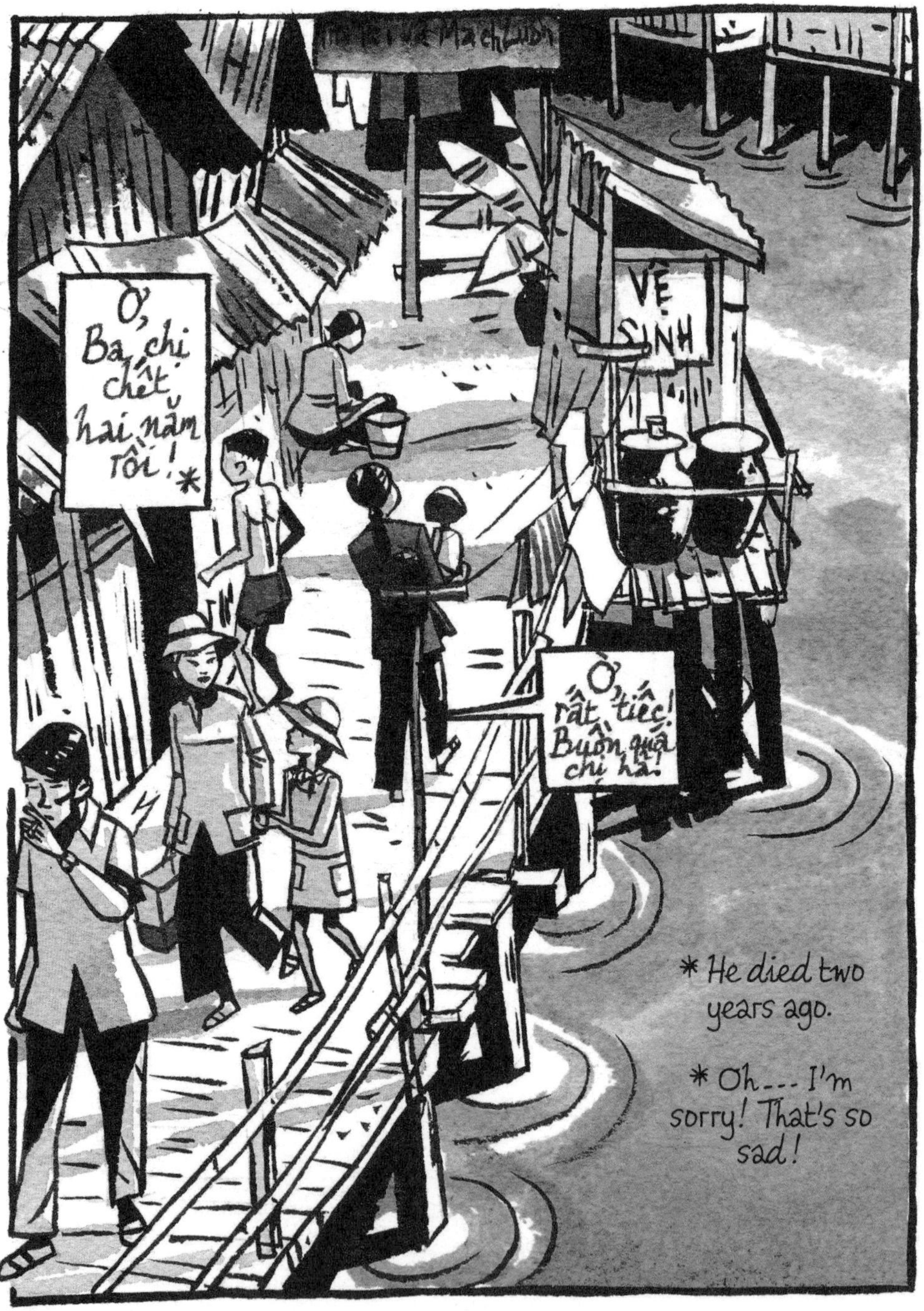
Ờ, Ba chị chết hai năm rồi! *
VỆ SINH
Ờ, rất tiếc! Buồn quá chị hả!
* He died two years ago.
* Oh--- I'm sorry! That's so sad!

To those who believed, Catholics and Communists promised paradise. The first got Heaven; the second, a radiant future and a plot of land ---

THE STRATEGIC HAMLETS

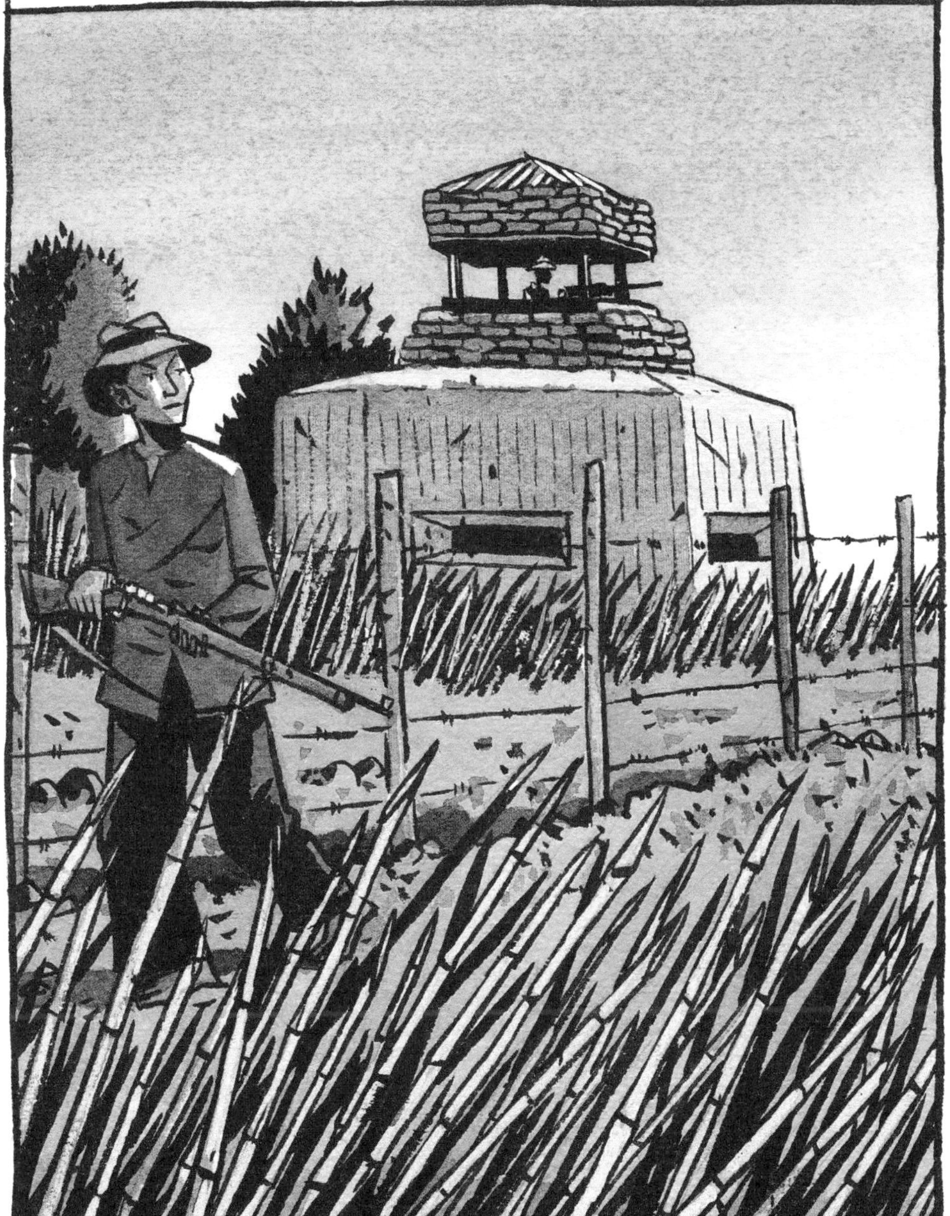

The big news in 1962 was the Strategic Hamlet Program, a spectacular project designed to eliminate Communist subversion.

A stamp was issued to mark the occasion. A lookout post, blockhouse, a perimeter drawn with sharp bamboo spikes and a pair of militiamen— not exactly Club Med!

Ngô Dinh Nhu, President Diêm's brother and main advisor, claimed to have invented the concept.

We are following the tradition of the village sheltered by bamboo ramparts.

Let's turn these fortified hamlets into cells of social and economic development!

The idea came from Mao's doctrine according to which the Communists were, or should be, in the population, "like a fish in water."

So we take the fish out of its water! We isolate the Viêt-Cong from the people by putting them safely behind a bamboo hedge.

UPI   M. Nhu   AFP NBC

Reuters

When night falls, anyone out in the countryside will be considered hostile and treated as such!

What do you mean by "considered hostile and treated as such," Mr. Advisor?

Those who are hostile to us will be treated the way the Communists treat their enemies.

Hundreds of fortified villages were built throughout the South. The population was forced to work on them.

The whole undertaking reminds me of the Kurosawa film "Seven Samurai," from 1954. A group of villagers are threatened by a horde of bandits, and seven mercenaries help them defend themselves by building a wall around the village, forming a militia, and fighting when it comes time to do battle.

The peasants of the delta *did* not at all appreciate being herded into fortified villages, torn from their lands and the graves of their ancestors. It was easy for the NLF to claim that the hamlets were internment camps where the people were held captive.

ĐẢ ĐẢO MỸ-DIỆM !!*

ĐẢ ĐẢO MỸ-DIỆM !

Not easy to contradict an armed man!

Agent of a NLF armed propaganda unit

The rural population was caught in the crossfire.

What a life! We slave for the rich by day, and labor for the Reds by night.

000

* Down with the American Diêmist regime!

Here is a propaganda sheet produced by the Saigon regime, the Republic of Vietnam. It reads, "The RVN's rural construction project will make the peasants' lives easier." But in fact, the Strategic Hamlet Program was a failure and it slowly faded away, but for a time, it was a stone in the Communists' path.

CHƯƠNG TRÌNH XÂY DỰNG NÔNG THÔN CỦA CHÍNH PHỦ V.N.C.H. NHẰM CẢI THIỆN ĐỜI SỐNG NÔNG DÂN

They took the threat very seriously, as this NLF poster attests: "Eradicate the Strategic Hamlets!" This 1962 piece of graphic art was the work of Huynh Van Gâm. Gâm and my father grew up in the same delta town in the South, and for a time they attended the same Saigon boarding school. Afterward, their paths separated.

TOTAL WAR

Reproduction of an anti-NLF propaganda sheet produced by the psychological warfare division of the Republic of Vietnam.

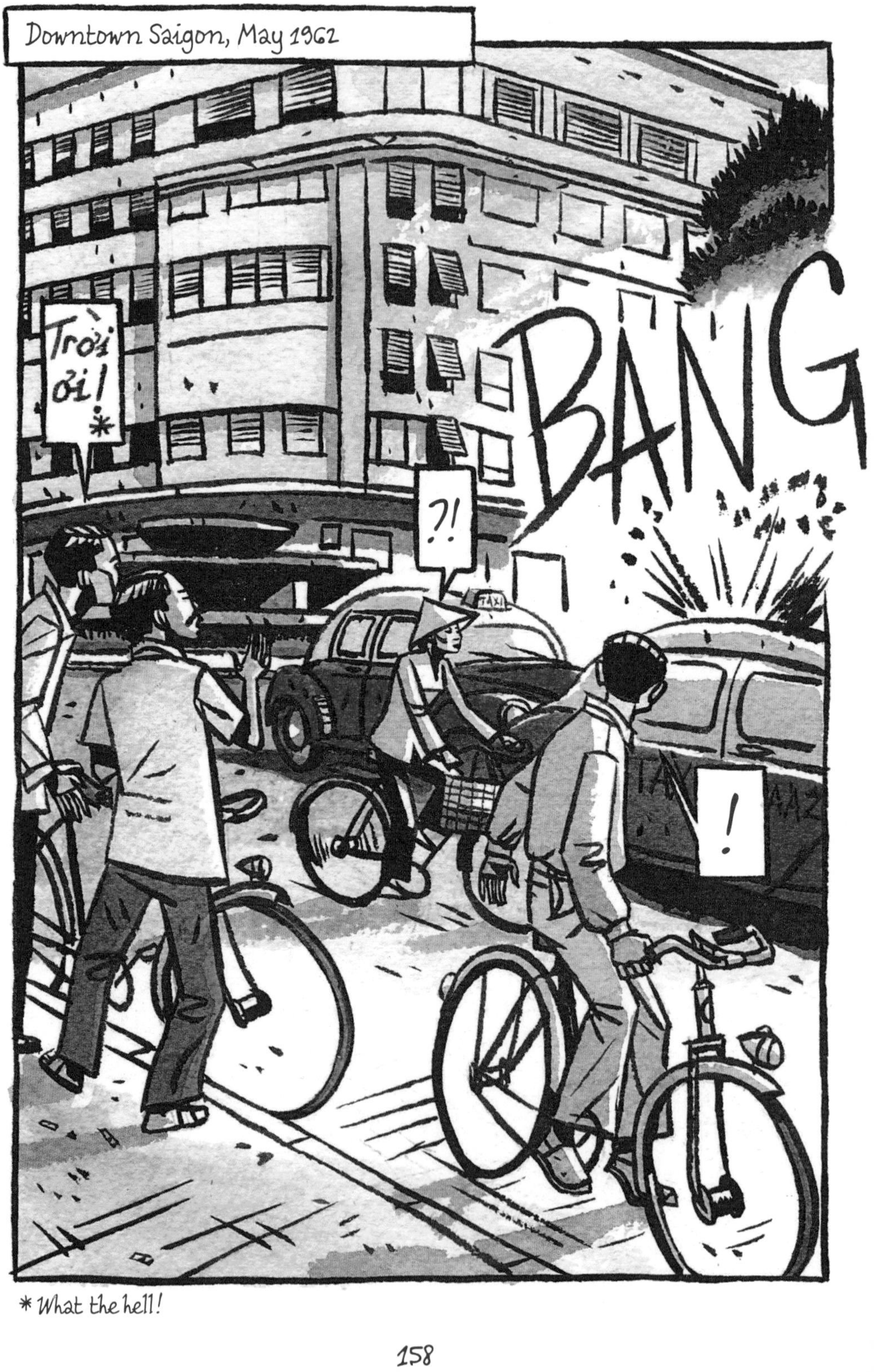
Downtown Saigon, May 1962
Trời ơi! *
BANG
?!
!

* What the hell!

In May 1962, a series of grenade attacks targeted places frequented by American advisors. There were about 2000 of them at the time.

June 1962. We were at the movies, laughing at Fernandel's antics in "Ali Baba and the 40 Thieves," when a grenade exploded in the moviehouse across from ours. Strangely, I have no memory of it.

The result: our trips to the movies were canceled. Mama was made for smoother seas ---

Fortunately, Chu Ba snuck us off to low-class movie theaters—no air conditioning! – that Americans avoided like the plague.

* The French songstress Dalida was very popular in Saigon.
* Four seats in the balcony.
160

We took in a lot of sword-and-sandals films: "Ben-Hur" for the culture, "Hercules" and the Maciste movies for the muscles.

* Who wants to buy fried bananas?!

Why did we love those costume dramas in Saigon? The good citizens must have recognized similarities between Caesar's Rome and Diêm's Saigon.

Like Caesar's centurions irritated by the Republic, our young Turks in camouflage conspired against the "Diêmocracy."*
There were always rumors of a coup d'état.

* "Diêmocracy" was a phrase coined by *Paris Match*.

One day Chu Ba came to our house, distress written all over his face.

* Are you sick, Chu Ba?   *No, not sick, Madame, just very sad.

Chu Ba told us that his brother-in-law, a test pilot at the Nha Trang training base, was killed when his plane crashed into the South China Sea.

* His widow, a mother of three, has suffered more pain than she can stand!

Mama had to give up on her idea of sending us to American school. American civilian and military advisors were flooding in. They would soon number 12,500.

With all those Americans, the prices will go up.

What will I do with my kids?

Three months' vacation! What a country!

Elvira

We had no problem ---

Get him, Khrushchev!

Kennedy, attack!

GLUB GLUB

YAY! I won!!

You two are so cruel!

Damn, my Kennedy ran away!

The Siamese fighting fish (Betta splendens) live in pools of fresh water in the rice paddies. When confined, two males will fight to the death which, in Vietnam, is an opportunity to lay bets.

Actually, there was nothing positive about the situation. Men and weapons continued to infiltrate the South on the Hô Chi Minh Trail, though the North insisted no such thing existed.

Hanoi refused to admit they were involved in the affairs of the South, and they tried to convince the world that the NLF rebellion was the work of "patriots" in the South. The land trail had its maritime double

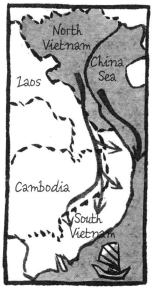

Hô Chi Minh Trail

A special unit was created in the center—the Junk Force*—to intercept infiltrators heading south.

* Lực Lượng Hải Thuyền

The motto of the Junk Force was "Sat Công": Kill Communists. Some sailors had the order tattooed on their chest. Better not get captured alive by the Viêt-Cong!

"Sat Công" was also the slogan of the Rangers, a special forces unit created in 1960 along American lines.

Uniform insignia of the South Vietnamese Rangers (Biêt Dong Quân)

"Kill Communists": a slogan worthy of a pesticide or an insecticide! This lack of taste was common in the anti-Communist camp. The Reds used better language. They brandished slogans that made people dream, words too good to be true.

VICTORY over the puppets will bring PEACE, FREEDOM, and democracy! We will carry out LAND REFORM!

Our strategy was as bad as our communications. The hardware that Uncle Sam dumped down on us was made for conventional warfare, and this was not that kind of war. We alienated the population.

* My rice paddies!

The iron armada, which grew enormously starting in 1965, caused all kinds of "collateral damage." (This euphemism was born during that period.)

* Murderers!

167

Starting in 1962, defoliants were used in the South. Vietnam's extensive vegetation provided ideal cover for the Viêt-Cong. "We'll get rid of it!" the Americans resolved, leading them to launch Operation Ranch Hand (1962-1970). Roadsides, outposts and riverbanks were defoliated with chem-icals delivered in enormous quantities.

This period marked the beginning of the use of Agent Orange. The term refers to the cocktail of defoliants dropped at dawn, before the heat of the day, since warm air rises and dis-perses the deadly orange cloud. Even today, in the "treated" areas, deformed children are being born because of this poison.

What *did* I know about chemical warfare in 1962? Nothing. Our side's propaganda contributed to the fear of the invisible enemy—the Viêt-Cong—but we had little information about what our government was really *doing*.

And our father? He had access to all sorts of information.

Saint-Malo, 2011

Papa, *did you know about the use of defoliants?*

Yes. But in 1962, the president's goal was to destroy the crops in the Viêt-Cong areas. He wanted to deprive the enemy of his means of subsistence.

The military thought they could limit ambushes by using defoliants around outposts, roads, and major rivers.

If you get rid of the forest, you can see your target better?

Yes, we wanted to cut our losses.

You know, Marcelino, we didn't consider the effect Agent Orange would have later.

THE TRUNG SISTERS MONUMENT

July 1962. We had been in Saigon a year. In her letters, Mama wrote about our little sister Anh-Noëlle growing up, and Papa "working himself to death," our endless breaks from school, the attacks in the city, and the incompetent help. She was weary in the extreme.

There were fights followed by reconciliation or sulking, as indicated by this enigmatic little story that Mireille (age 11) added to a letter to our Saint-Malo grandparents.

Monsieur and Madame are at quiet war with each other. For a week, they haven't spoken, but since life has to go on anyway, they exchange little notes. One evening, Monsieur puts a note on the bedside table: "Wake me tomorrow at seven." The next day, he woke at 9 and found a note: "Wake up, it's seven."

One day, in one full swoop, Mama fired our maids: Chi Hai and her sister Chi Ba who had come as back-up. Mama called them filthy, thieving, incapable, stupid, backward ...

Much later, we learned their father wasn't dead. He had simply disappeared. In 1975, he showed up: he was a captain in the People's Army. The war was also the rebellion of the servant class.

Papa, did you know that Chi Hai and Chi Ba's father was in the Viêt-Cong?

Yes. My mother told me about it. She was close to their mother.

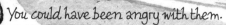

You could have been angry with them.

Not at all! All Vietnamese were close to someone in the resistance. Take my cousin Ai. He was Viêt-Cong and the whole family knew.

One of my paternal grandmother's older brothers married a very rich woman. Their three sons were raised in the lap of luxury. Ai, the youngest, was always accompanied by a domestic.

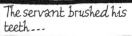

The servant brushed his teeth---

Tchic Tchic

He dressed him---

--- and carried him on his back for any trip longer than a few meters!

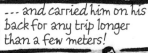

In 1945, seduced by the egalitarian ideals of the Revolution, Ai joined the Viêt-Minh---*

Farewell, master!

--- only to reappear 30 years later, at the end of the war,* wearing the uniform of a People's Army major.

* The Communist resistance movement fighting the French.

* 1975: the end of the Vietnam War (1959–75).

October 1962. On the Bach Dang quay, right by our house, the people of Saigon had a new subject of conversation: the regime's monument to the Trung Sisters.*

The teacher told us how the Trung Sisters defeated the Chinese with an army of women in the year 40 A.D. blah blah blah---

I'm the sister watching the northern frontier!

BORING! I'd rather eat fried bananas!

* People said Trung Trac, facing the south, defended the southern border while her sister Trung N'hi kept watch over the Communists in the North.

175

People whispered that Madame Nhu and her daughter Lê-Thuy had posed as the two national heroines for sculptor Paul Nguyen Van The.

I don't know if it's true. But in March 1963, a stamp was issued in honor of the Trung Sisters Monument, and on the stamp, Madame Nhu and Lê-Thuy figure prominently.

Public opinion questioned the right of Madame Nhu to appropriate the national myth of the Trung Sisters.

October 26, 1962, on the national holiday commemorating the 7th anniversary of the Republic of Vietnam, the new combat helicopter delivered by Uncle Sam—the famous Bell UH-1H Iroquois, nicknamed the "Huey"—was displayed in front of City Hall.

The chopper would become the emblem of the Vietnam War. It was supposed to tip the balance in favor of Saigon. But to show they weren't backing down, the VC threw two grenades in two places in the crowd, killing six and wounding dozens.

Six dead and thirty-seven wounded? Nothing compared to the damage that the gunships would cause in the years to come. But the Communists' message was clear.

Papa and Mama were in the crowd at City Hall. A letter from Mama dated October 30, 1962, describing the fireworks on our holidays:

The armaments the Americans are deploying here certainly impress the other side. There was a grenade in the middle of the show of American weaponry 200 meters from our house, with 6 dead and 37 wounded! Fortunately, I've noticed that they throw grenades in certain favorite spots, and that there aren't many of them (too many searches!), and only on holidays. The Vietnamese sergeant who was hit lay down on it instead of throwing it further into the crowd. The Army is disciplined. The soldiers look proud. The crowd was dense on October 26, happy and pushing forward. Five minutes after the grenade, they were back. People are eager for any distraction.

The attacks caused fear, but the mop came out and life went back to normal. We were lucky in town. The real war was in the countryside. From time to time, to convince the citizens we were going to win, the government displayed its hunting trophies.

I remember a strange spectacle in the middle of downtown --- A display of weapons captured from the Viêt-Cong, trophies of this lovely little war.

In the square in front of the National Assembly, weapons of all caliber and origins were lined up, identified by labels.

For esthetic reasons, areca palms were set here and there. Parachutes provided shade. NLF flags added a splash of color.

* The nickname of the 12.7 caliber Soviet machine gun, the Degtyaryov-Shpagin (DShK 1938).

I can still hear the soldier with the megaphone. His voice bit into the air.

These weapons were seized at great cost from the Viêt-Cong aggressors supported by Hanoi!

!!

These sorts of demonstrations were meant to galvanize the population and make it believe in its army.

Well, if we managed to get our hands on that hardware, the Viêt-Cong must have ten times more!

Chiên Lợi Phẩm
Chiên Dịch
Dân Tiến 27

Chiên Loi Phâm: spoils of war; Chiên Dich: campaign; Dân Thiên 27: the people advancing 27

181

The show's top attraction was a 37mm Soviet anti-aircraft cannon, a legend of Russia's Great Patriotic War (1941-1945) that had somehow found its way to South Vietnam. Now the cannon was a fairgrounds attraction. Like the other kids, I lined up to sit on one of the tractor seats on the ride. My own childhood merry-go-round.

I got *dibs* on the shooter's seat!

Hey, I want it too!

But I'm older and bigger!

Cái này không đẹp, Chú Ba!*

Đúng, cái này không đẹp.

* I don't like those things, Chu Ba.   No, neither do I!

182

Should children have been kept away from that kind of display?
Actually, the Saigon regime was competing with Hanoi. In the North,
the Communist state, forged by warfare with France during the First
Indochina War (1946-1954), had militarized its society and didn't
think twice about placing a rifle—even if it was a replica—in a
child's hands.

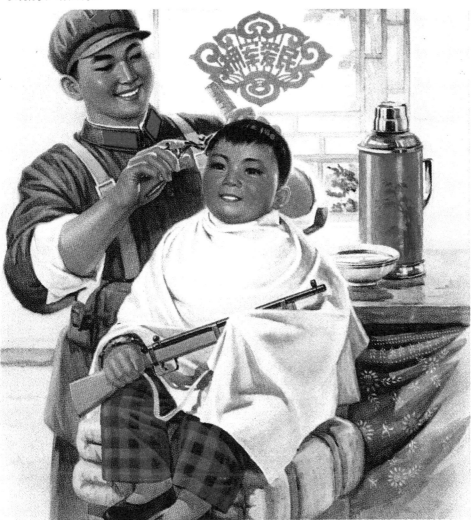

The Vietnamese Communists followed Maoist thought to the letter. The
child must prepare himself to become a soldier in the People's Army, like
in this propaganda image that reminds me of the barbers in Saigon.
They would blow on the back of your neck to cool down the burn from
their shears.

When it suited them, the Communists claimed to be pacifists, but actually, they were ultra-militarists. Compared to them, we Saigon "puppets" were dilettantes. We were much less brainwashed. Unfortunately, since our bombs did not distinguish between men and women, adults and children, soldiers and civilians, we ended up creating an endless chain of fanatic enemies of both sexes, determined to avenge their dead.

In the NLF, all-female units took part in the fighting. There are numerous paintings and examples of war art featuring these women guerrillas. They are often associated with the lotus, whose root reaches down into the mud and whose flower, the symbol of purity, opens toward the sky. I wonder what it must have been like to come up against a unit like that and have to open fire on them.

THE BATTLE OF ÂP BAC

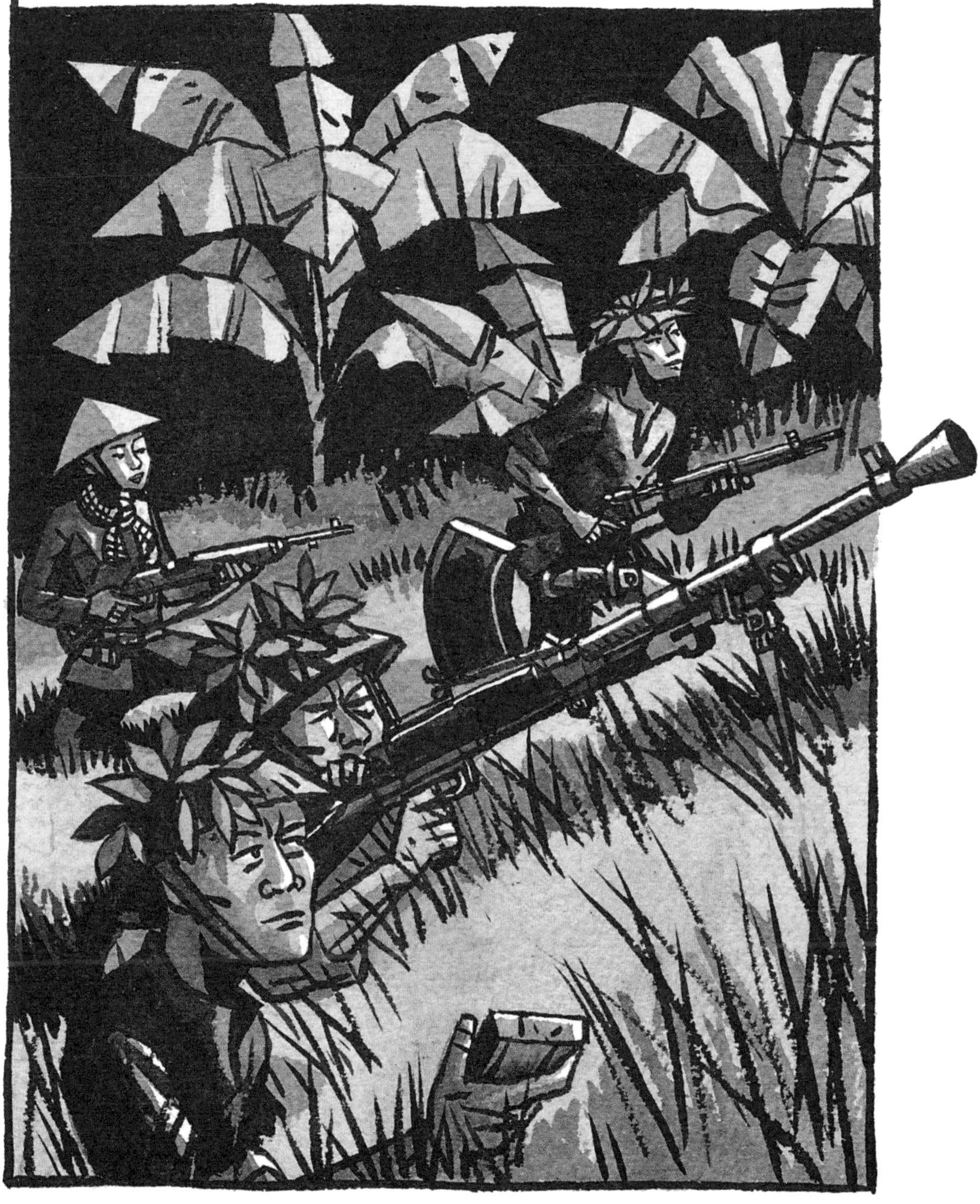

As the Christians' Christmas grew near, our boulevard filled up with trees and manger scenes.

The shop displays overflowed with cheap, made-in-Hong Kong toys.

No attacks. You would have thought an unspoken truce had been declared, and even dream of a merry Christmas.

But the truce was short and 1963 began with a defeat. The Army of the Republic of Vietnam carried out an operation 65 km from Saigon, with copters, planes, armor, artillery, paratroopers, and ground troops—just to dislodge 300 Viêt-Cong from the village of Áp Bac. Our side had picked up their radio signal.

There were five Army troops for every one VC. But the VC put up fierce resistance. Their determination was relentless.

I'll spare you the details of what happened at Âp Bac. Imagine a day-long battle, with bullets and shrapnel lacerating flesh---

--- breaking bones ---

---perforating muscles and chopping off limbs.

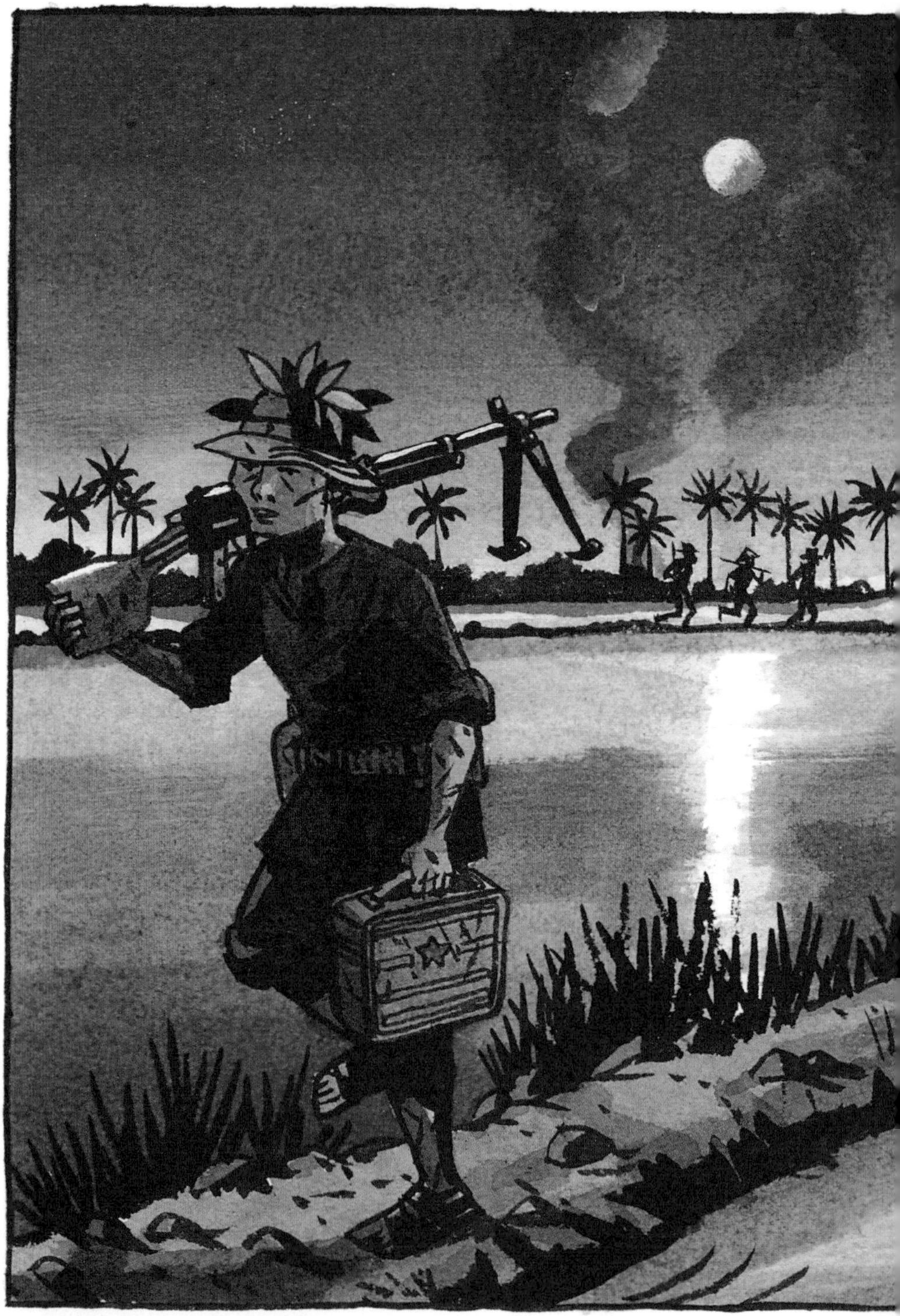

Under cover of night, the Viêt-Cong escaped through the flooded rice paddies, slipping through holes in the net like a moray eel in the open sea.

It was a fiasco for our troops; their commanders weren't up to snuff. Sixty-five of our soldiers and three American advisors were killed. There were only some twenty Viêt-Cong bodies.

I can't believe they had so few losses!

The VC never leave their dead in the field when they can help it.

A third of the choppers sent by the Americans were disabled. Clearly, the VC had found a way to neutralize the weapon that was supposed to tip the balance in our favor. The victor was a great coup for VC propaganda.

The worst thing is that my Vietnamese soldiers lost face. They know how to fight when they're led right.

You're not the only one saying that.

↗American advisor   ↖ Neil Sheehan, from the news agency UPI

192

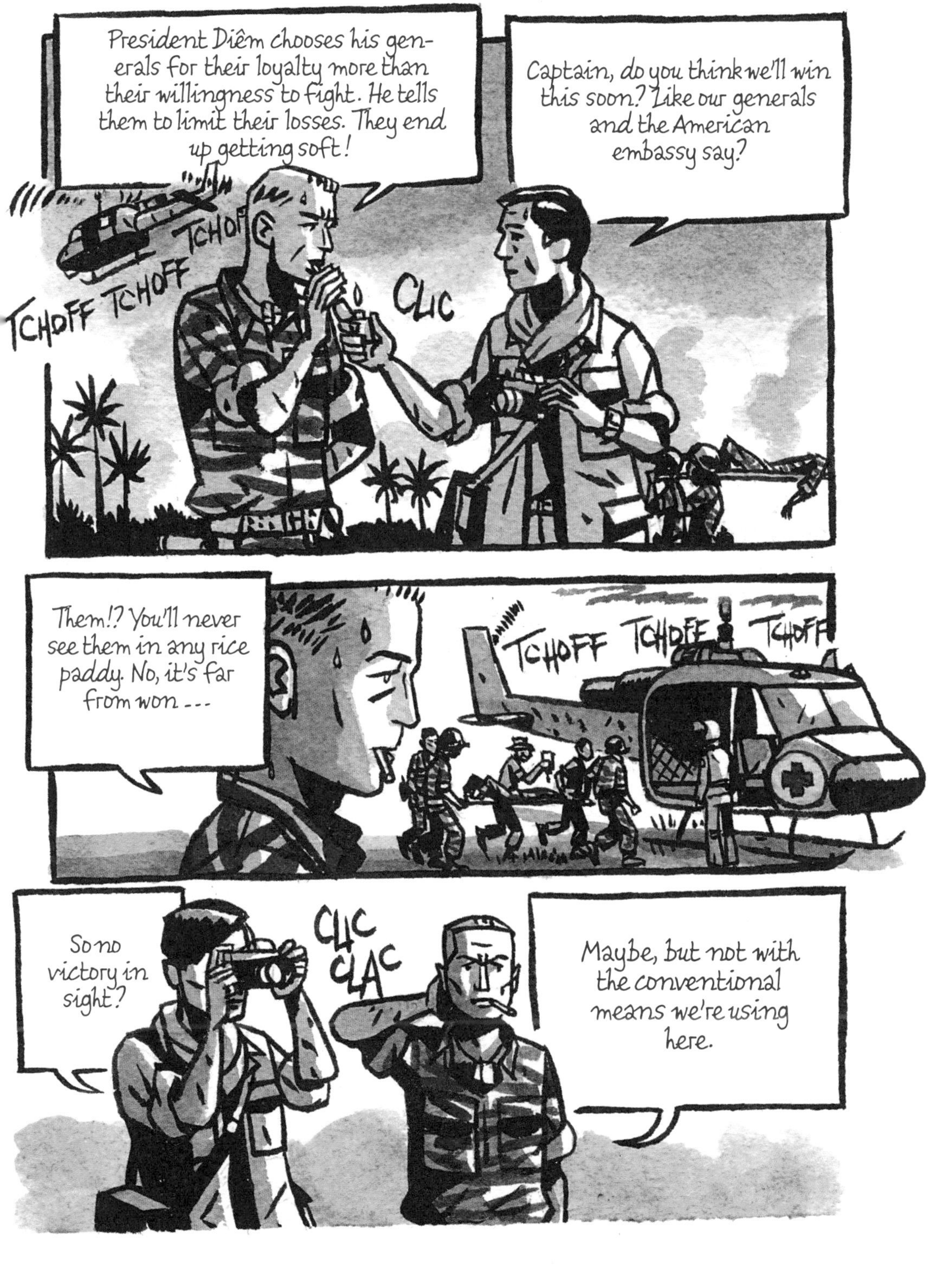
President Diêm chooses his generals for their loyalty more than their willingness to fight. He tells them to limit their losses. They end up getting soft!
TCHOFF TCHOFF TCHOFF
CLIC
Captain, do you think we'll win this soon? Like our generals and the American embassy say?
Them!? You'll never see them in any rice paddy. No, it's far from won ---
TCHOFF TCHOFF TCHOFF
So no victory in sight?
CLIC CLAC
Maybe, but not with the conventional means we're using here.

CLIC CLAC

This isn't Bastogne or Guadalcanal. This is a new kind of conflict. A revolutionary war, a war of subversion.

The Viêt-Cong aren't fighting to occupy territory. Not yet --- Right now they want to win the hearts and minds of the population.

They've blended into the population, and our tanks, planes, and cannons aren't much use because of it. We need to identify the enemy within the population and eliminate him cleanly, with this!

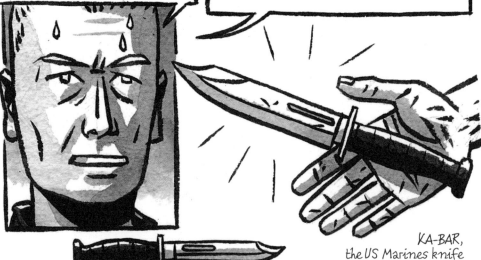

KA-BAR, the US Marines knife

We got our asses whipped here. All our hardware didn't change a thing.

TCHOFF
TCHOFF
TCHOFF

You can be sure that the Saigon brass is going to claim victory and say we're winning this lousy war!

That's the kind of music Washington wants to hear. But you journalists can set the record straight about what's happening on the ground!

The next day, at the HQ of General Paul Harkins, commander of the American Military Assistance Command—Vietnam.

Mr. President, the Viêt-Cong cut and ran, and abandoned their position. A great victory!

Washington. The Oval Office in the White House.

That's not what I'm reading in the *New York Times*, Paul. The *Times* says we got beat badly! You sure we're talking about the same war?

During the entire war, there was a gap between the triumphant tone of the high command and a more pessimistic picture of the conflict painted by the American press.

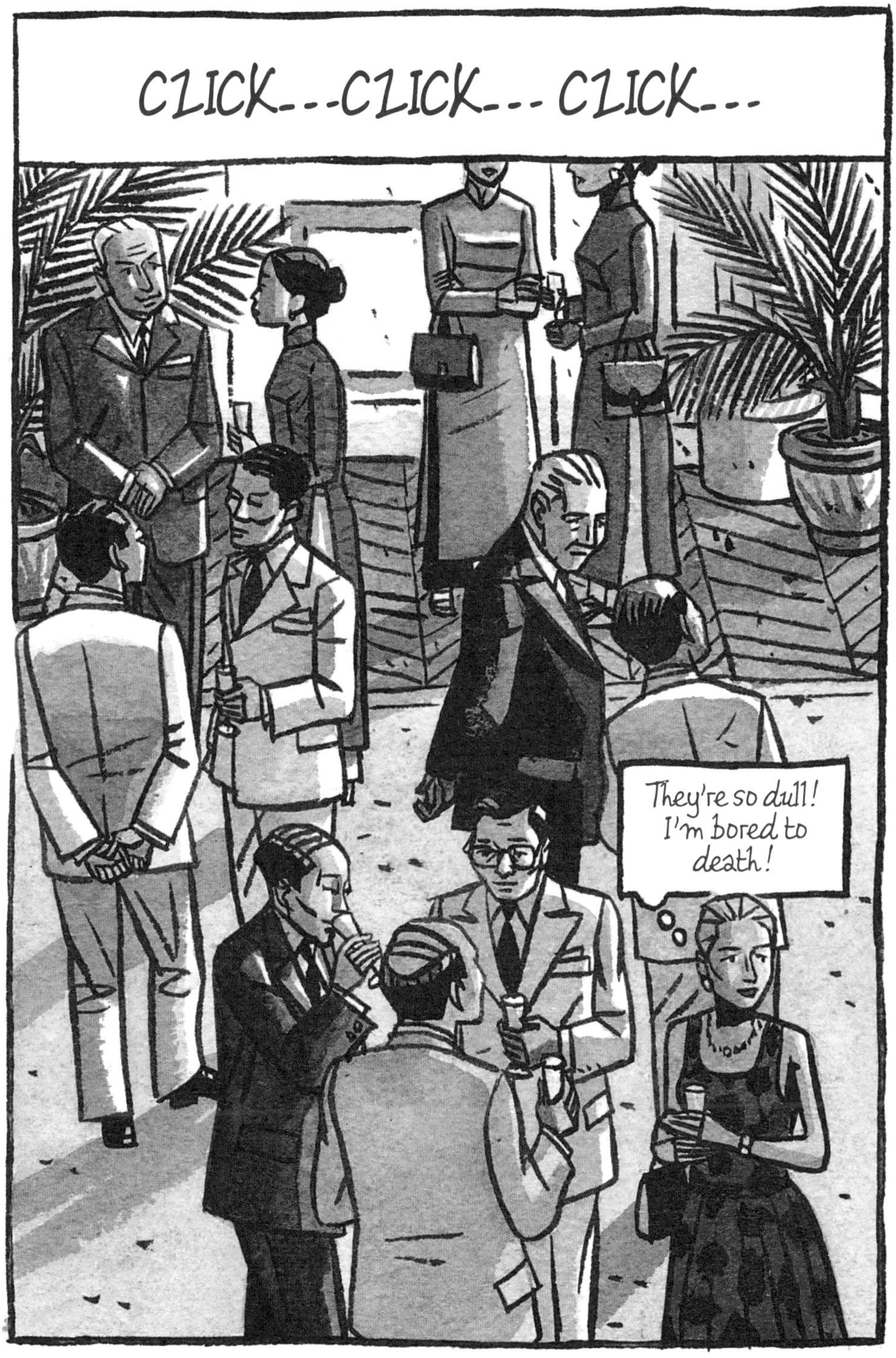
CLICK---CLICK--- CLICK---
They're so dull! I'm bored to death!

High society life went on ---

By describing Ấp Bắc as a defeat for our troops, the American press stabbed us in the back!

President Diêm is in a rage!

American journalists are hurting us, but American democracy is based on freedom of the press.

Sure, but our country is at war!

The Communists don't have to worry about criticism from a free press!

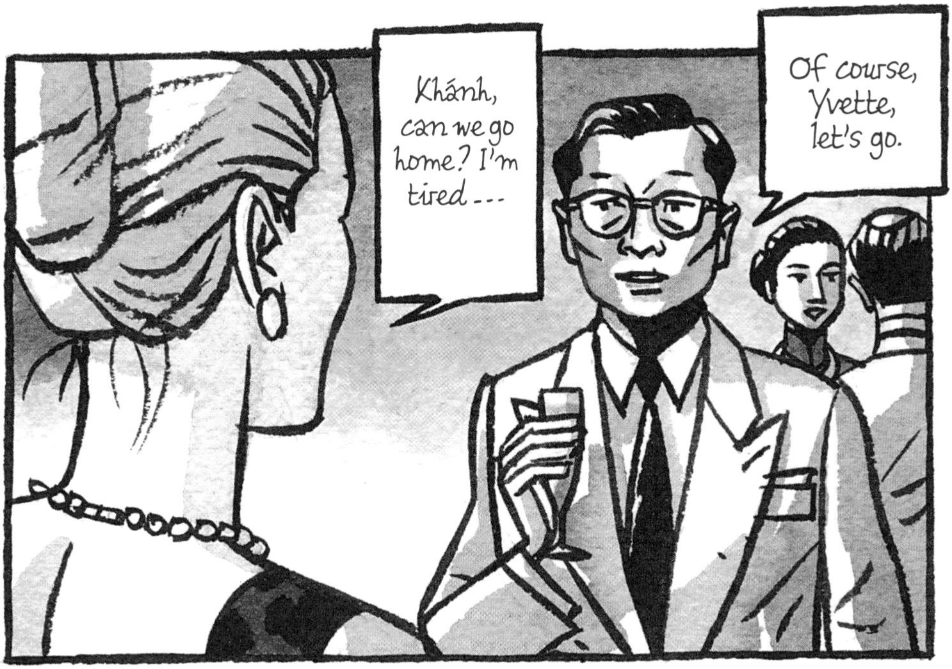
Khánh, can we go home? I'm tired ...
Of course, Yvette, let's go.

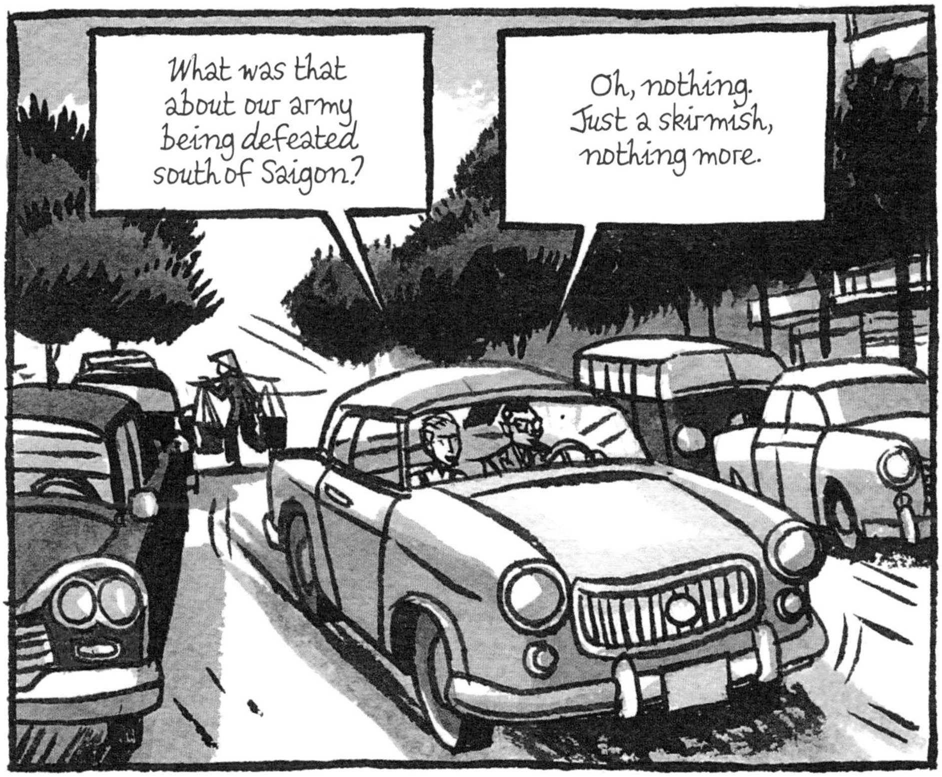
What was that about our army being defeated south of Saigon?
Oh, nothing. Just a skirmish, nothing more.

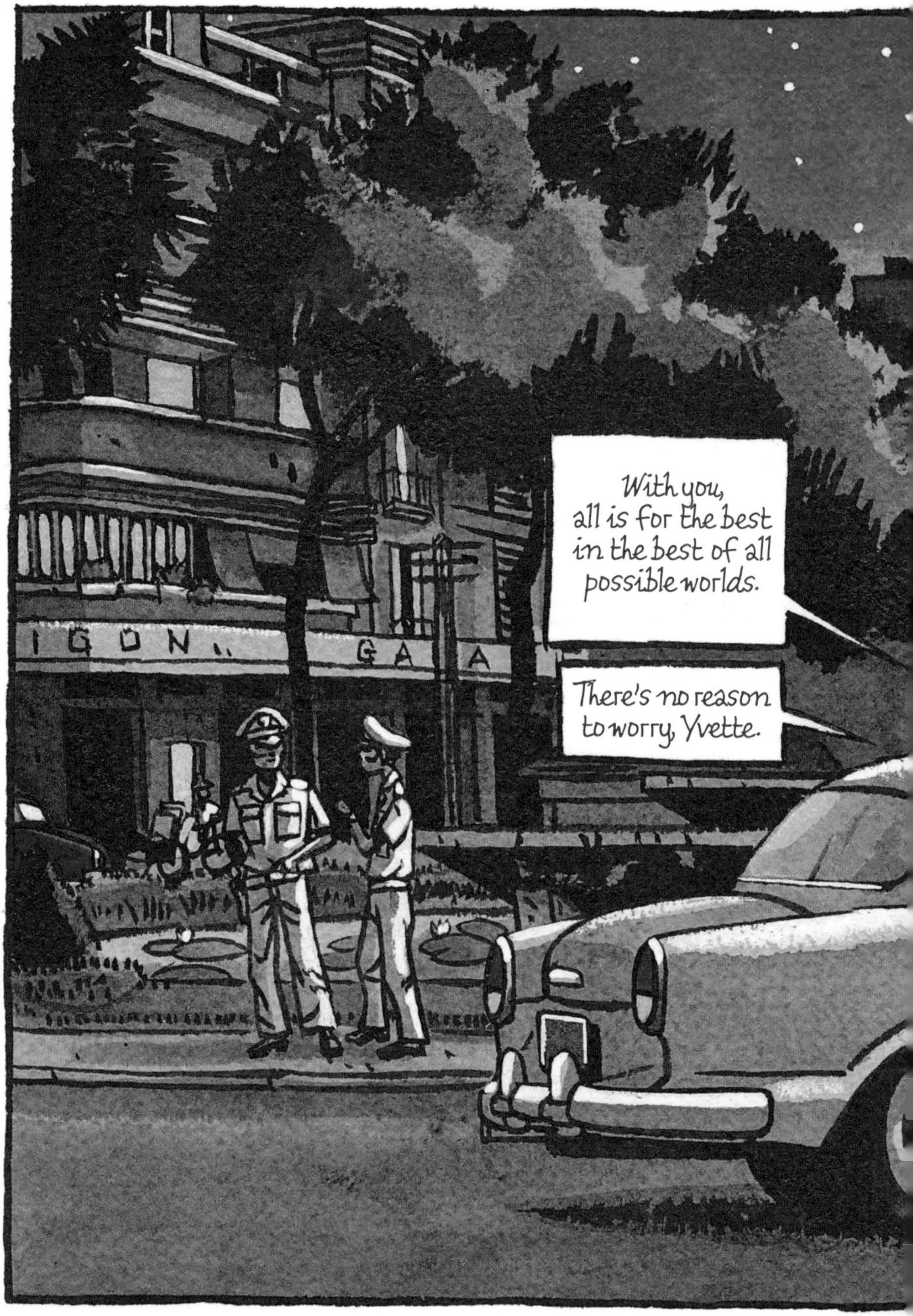
IGON
GA A
With you, all is for the best in the best of all possible worlds.
There's no reason to worry, Yvette.

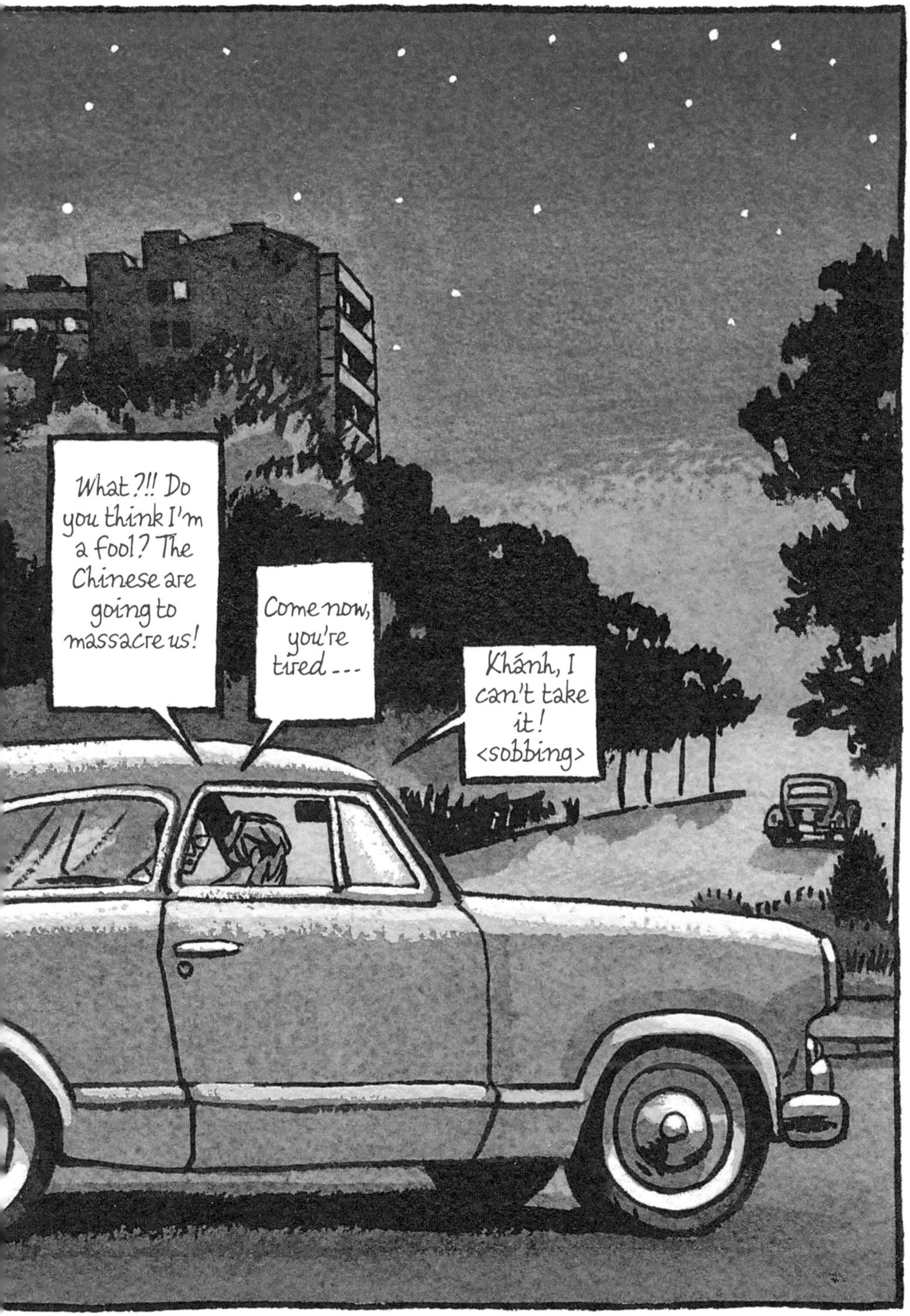
What?!! Do you think I'm a fool? The Chinese are going to massacre us!
Come now, you're tired ---
Khánh, I can't take it! <sobbing>

Around this time, Mama came back from the market with a strange creature.

Ick, it looks like a prehistoric beast!

It's a horseshoe crab. People here eat it on the barbecue. They eat anything!

Trời đất ơi! *
Are we going to eat this monster?

Oh, no, I just wanted to show it to you ---

SWIIIISH

CLICK

* Heaven and earth!

202

For a few more minutes, the dying horseshoe crab slapped against the floor with its tail, then stopped ---

In Saigon, we were sheltered from the worst, but the country was sinking into war. I remember, just as I was falling asleep, how I would feel a fear I could not name.

Oh, I hate that. My heart is beating like a drum!

POM PAM   POM PAM

Awkwardly, I tried to talk about it, but in vain.

Mireille, does my heart keep beating during the night?

Of course it does, silly! If it didn't beat, you'd be dead.

Hee hee!

I was afraid, especially at night. Maybe because of the rumors that predicted a bloodbath if the Communists took over.

Our cousins Buu Diên and Buu Dai came over to play sometimes. Buu Diên's joke gives you an idea of the atmosphere.

The meetings of the Famous Three took place in the bathroom (in case of fire!).

Ô Pater auster, Mater dolorosa et spiritu sanctu!

Shh, Marco! The Câu lac bô* is meeting!

The spirits are about to speak!

* club.

??!

Ick! A cockroach!! There!

!?

Horseshoe crab tail + coconut half-shell = Marco's sword

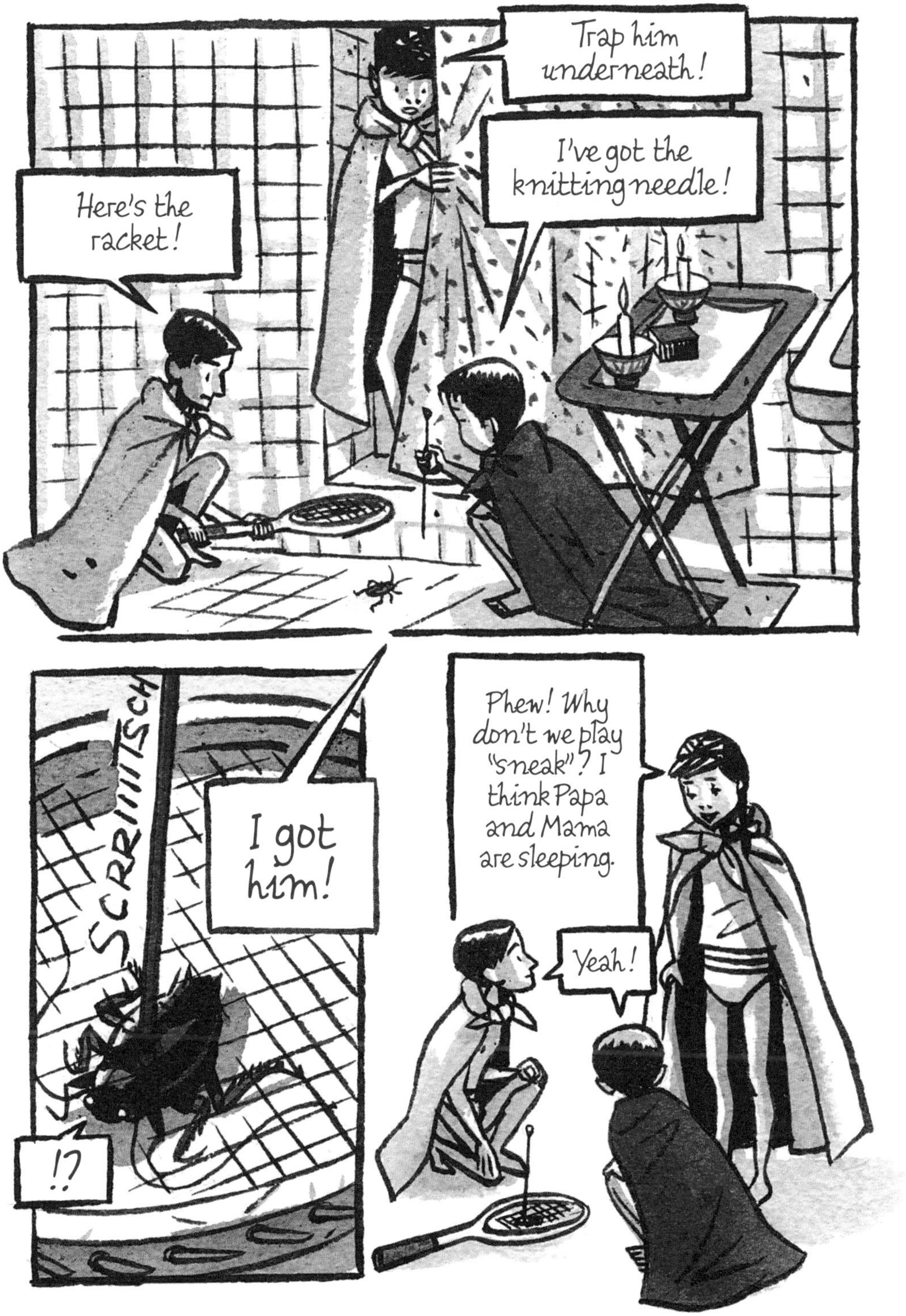
Here's the racket!
Trap him underneath!
I've got the knitting needle!
SCRRIIIITSCH
I got him!
!?
Phew! Why don't we play "sneak"? I think Papa and Mama are sleeping.
Yeah!

One of our favorite games involved sneaking through the apartment when our parents thought we were asleep in our beds. We called it "sneak," a word we brought with us from the United States.

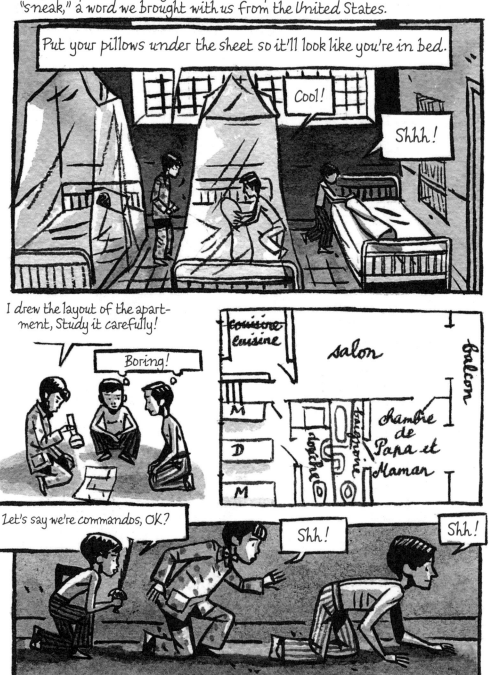

That night, we were secret witnesses to Mama's breakdown...

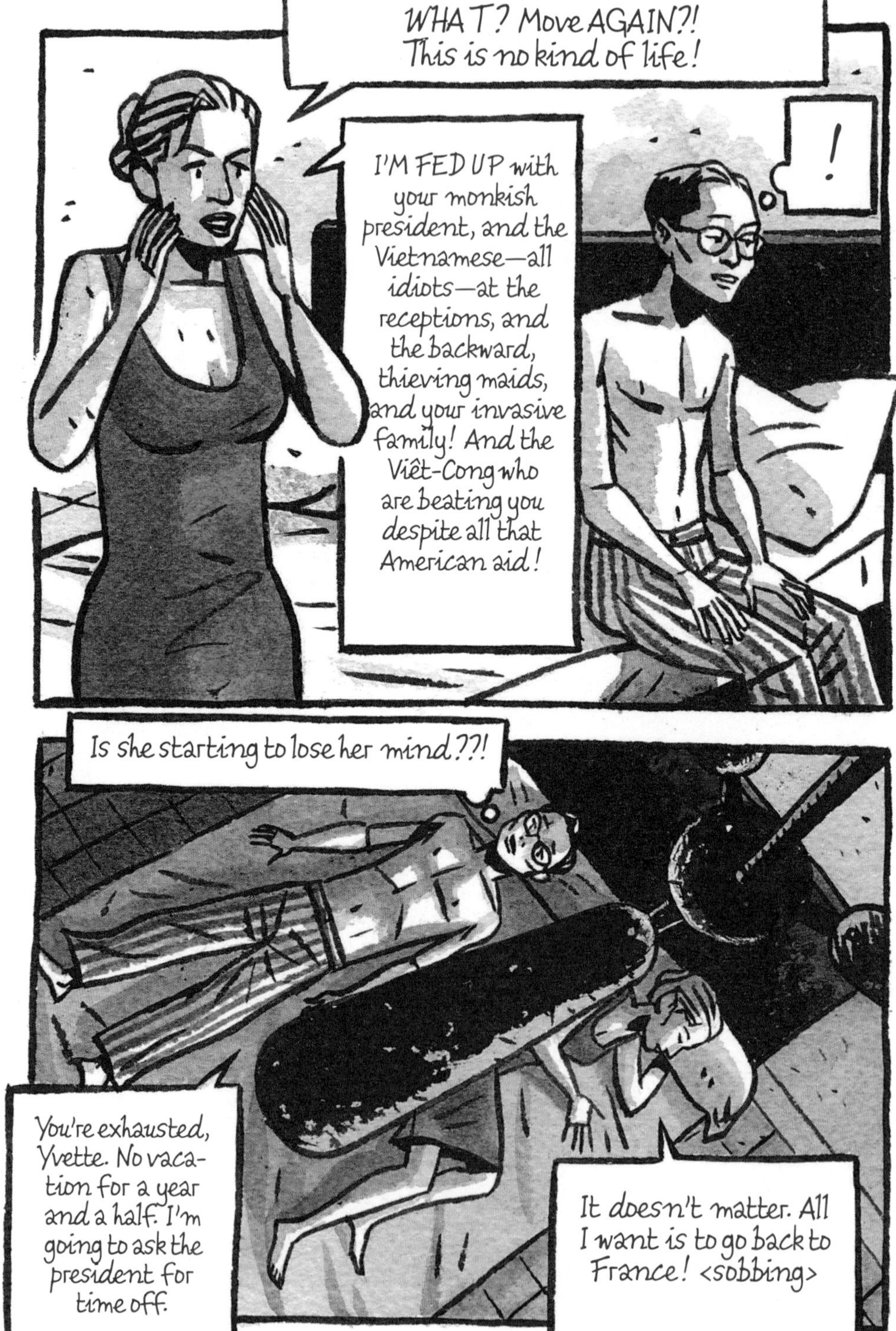
WHAT? Move AGAIN?! This is no kind of life!
I'M FED UP with your monkish president, and the Vietnamese—all idiots—at the receptions, and the backward, thieving maids, and your invasive family! And the Viêt-Cong who are beating you despite all that American aid!
!
Is she starting to lose her mind??!
You're exhausted, Yvette. No vacation for a year and a half. I'm going to ask the president for time off.
It doesn't matter. All I want is to go back to France! <sobbing>

GREETINGS FROM NHA TRANG

At the end of March 1963, we took a plane to Nha Trang for a vacation. Someone lent us a house on a promontory overlooking the bay. The site was magnificent. Emperor Bao Dai* had built a villa there.

Is that our house?

No, that's the Bao Dai villa. Ours is lower down.

Wow, the sea is so blue!

To the north, the bay of Nha Trang, with six miles of soft sand. To the south, a pretty inlet accessible by a stairway made of tall stone steps.

Mireille, Domi, you think there are VC in the bushes?

You mean WC or VC?

* The last Annam emperor, Bao Dai, reigned from 1926 to 1945.

I mean
Viêt-Cong!

Of course
not!

?

What are
you boys
talking
about?!!

Nothing, nothing,
Mãma!!

Stop quarreling!
Look at this beauty. It's like paradise!

The setting was idyllic, but after a brief euphoria, Mother's mood changed.

This house is un-be-lieve-ably filthy! It needs airing out! It hasn't been cleaned since 1954!* It's DIS-GUST-ING!

Chu Ba will come and clean tomorrow.

To help Mother, Chu Ba and Chi Hai took the bus and joined us. Papa wanted to spare her from being overworked.

I've never been to the sea!

Me neither!

Let's hope Madame is in a good mood.

But Madame wasn't in a good mood. And Papa had to go back to work.

What am I going to do all alone with four children?

The president is calling. I have to go.

Chu Ba and Chi Hai will help you.

* 1954: the end of the war in Indochina. The French leave.

Luckily, Chu Ba and Chi Hai were there during the month we spent in Nha Trang.

I remember a sort of tribal dance we invented.
I still have the Chinese music in my head.

US Army entrenching tool

One day, we went out on a boat.
A flock of junks with bat wings was
moving out to sea.

Wow,
that's cool!

Những chiếc ghe này
là gì vậy, chú Ba?*

* What are those junks doing, Chu Ba?!

Đó là Lực Lượng Hải Thuyền ra chận không cho Bắc Việt đưa súng ống vô đây. *

* That's the "Junk Force" stopping the infiltration of weapons from the North.

Hành dinh của họ ở Nha Trang. Cháu biết khẩu hiệu của họ không? Là "Sát Cộng"! *

Sát Cộng! Sát Cộng!

?!

Sát Cộng! Sát Cộng!

* Their headquarters are in Nha Trang. You know their motto? "Kill the Reds!"

If only we could stop teaching him those terrible things! Quiet, Marco!

218

WANDERING SOULS

Chérie je t'aime, chérie je t'adore! ♪♫

Chờ một chút! Chú đã bỏ quên gói thuốc lá ở nhà. *

Đừng lo, cháu sẽ bảo vệ chú! *

* Just a minute, I forgot my cigarettes at my place. * OK, I'll cover you!

Chu Ba, his wife, and their six children were all crammed into tight servants' quarters at the back of our building.

* Hello, Marco, what are you doing?

*Hello, Madame! I'm going for a walk.

Chu Ba's salary wasn't enough to feed his family. He had a way of making a little extra that was not without danger.

How much was a liter of blood worth? Were rare blood types better paid? How much blood did you give in one go? I have no idea.

Poor Chu Ba! He was always so nice to us --- After we left, the army finally caught up to him.

He was assigned to the front of an armored train.

I don't know if Chu Ba survived the war. I wanted to look for him, but I didn't know his real name.

I wonder if Chu Ba is here somewhere?

In 1991, I visited the main cemetery of the army of South Vietnam, in Biên Hoa, near Saigon. The Communists had let the place go to ruin. Sixteen thousand "puppets" were buried there. At the top of an overgrown hill, a Chinese-style monument held the Tomb of the Unknown Soldier.

Woe to the conquered!

225

The Unknown Soldier's tomb was empty ---

They raided the grave. What did they do with the body?

As I stepped around the vandalized tomb, my heart leaped.

Oh! What's that?!

It was as if the Unknown Soldier, expelled from his tomb, were sleeping his ghostly sleep elsewhere ---

Jesus, he's breathing!

He must be homeless. He has a brush cut, like Chu Ba.

Without waking him, I slipped a few banknotes under a stone by his callused hands.

It's getting dark.
Better get out of here!
Give the place back to the
wandering souls.

228

THE BUDDHIST CRISIS

* Homage to Buddha Amitabha ---

At the beginning of May 1963, an important political crisis developed in Huê, in central Vietnam. Buddhism was the majority religion in the country, practiced by moderates. Feeling persecuted by President Diêm, who was suspected of favoring the Catholic minority, the bonzes of Huê called for demonstrations. The response was violent repression: live ammunition, grenades ...

The demonstrations reached Saigon in June. The bonzes became the de facto spokesmen of all enemies of the Diêm regime, unpopular and challenged.

* Down with the American Diêm regime!!

Faced with the challenge, the Ngô clan closed ranks.

Ngô Dinh Diêm

This kind of opposition would never be tolerated in the North, Mr. Nolting. I have the world's journalists on my back.

United States ambassador, F. Nolting

The bonzes are being manipulated by the Communists. Let's not be naïve!

Ngô Dinh Nhu

Disorder is just what the Viêt-Cong want. Any excuse to destabilize the South!

Madame Nhu

Today we know the Buddhist protest movement was infiltrated by Communists, who fed the flames of discontent.

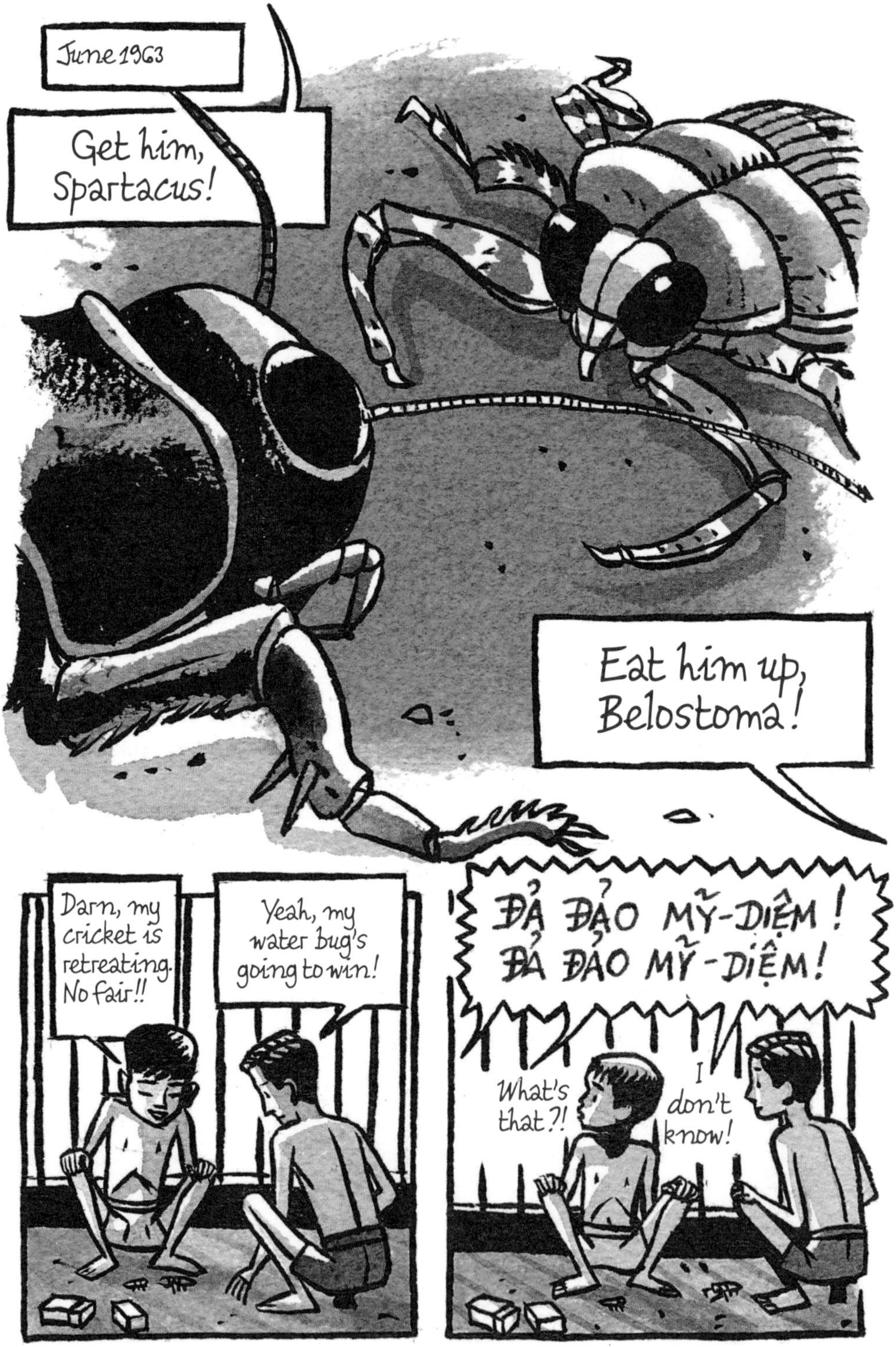
June 1963
Get him, Spartacus!
Eat him up, Belostoma!
Darn, my cricket is retreating. No fair!!
Yeah, my water bug's going to win!
ĐẢ ĐẢO MỸ-DIỆM!
ĐẢ ĐẢO MỸ-DIỆM!
What's that?!
I don't know!

* *The pheromone of giant water bugs is used to flavor certain Vietnamese dishes.*

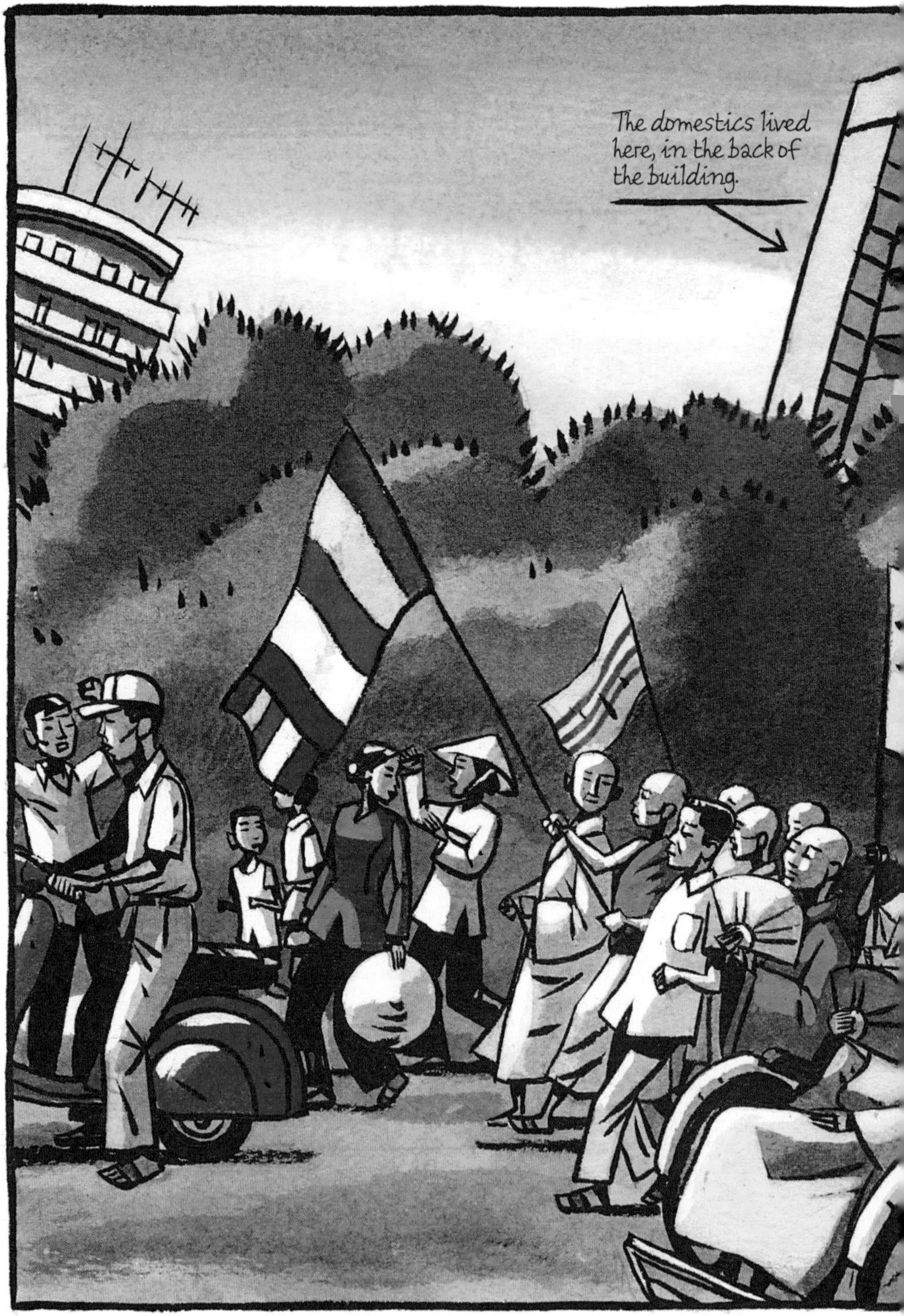
The domestics lived here, in the back of the building.

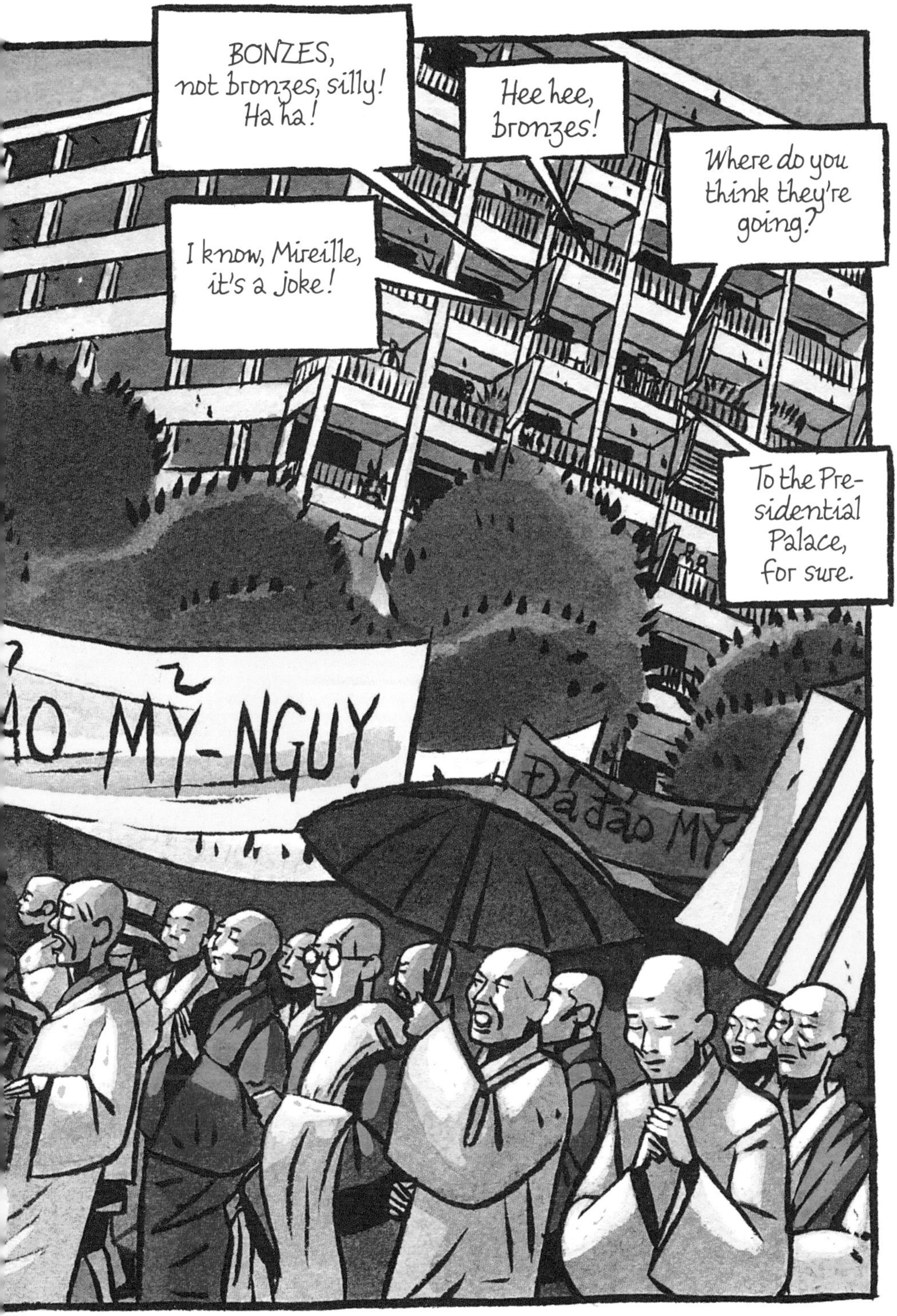
BONZES, not bronzes, silly! Ha ha!
Hee hee, bronzes!
I know, Mireille, it's a joke!
Where do you think they're going?
To the Presidential Palace, for sure.
ĐẢ ĐẢO MỸ-NGUY!
ĐẢ ĐẢO MỸ-

A few days later, I was hit with a high fever. Mama feared the worst. There had been cases of the plague.

* Hôpital Grall? We can do that, Madame!

What a mess! Everything's blocked!

TOOT TOO

HOOT HOOOT

The smell of something charred filled the streets blocked by a giant traffic jam.

What's that burning? Is it the car, Chu Ba?

Good Lord, we're stuck! HONK YOUR HORN!

Tôi không hiểu! Không hiểu!

* I don't understand!

A few hundred yards from the intersection where we were stuck, a bonze named Thich Quang Duc set himself on fire. Foreign correspondents had been tipped off. One of them, Malcolm Browne,* took the pictures that were published around the world, tolling the death-knell for the Diêm regime.

*Malcolm Browne was the director of the Associated Press (AP) in Saigon.

In a letter to her parents after the spectacular auto-da-fé, Mama was no doubt shocked, but she avoided the subject.

My dear parents,   18 June, 1963
   I'm writing so you won't be worried, since you probably heard about the Buddhist demonstration that took place in Saigon last week.
   We're getting over our emotions, and the flu, but today everyone is in good spirits again.

My fever wasn't the onset of the plague, and soon I was well enough to play with fire.

July 1963

Mama, are we going to see Ông Nội and Bà Nội* this afternoon?

No. Your grandfather said Bà Nội was going to the Xa-Lôi pagoda.

Really? Why? She's not Buddhist.

?!

Not at all, Bà Nội is very Catholic ---

I know why! Bà Nội went to see Thich Quang Duc's heart.

What?!

* Our paternal grandparents

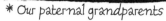

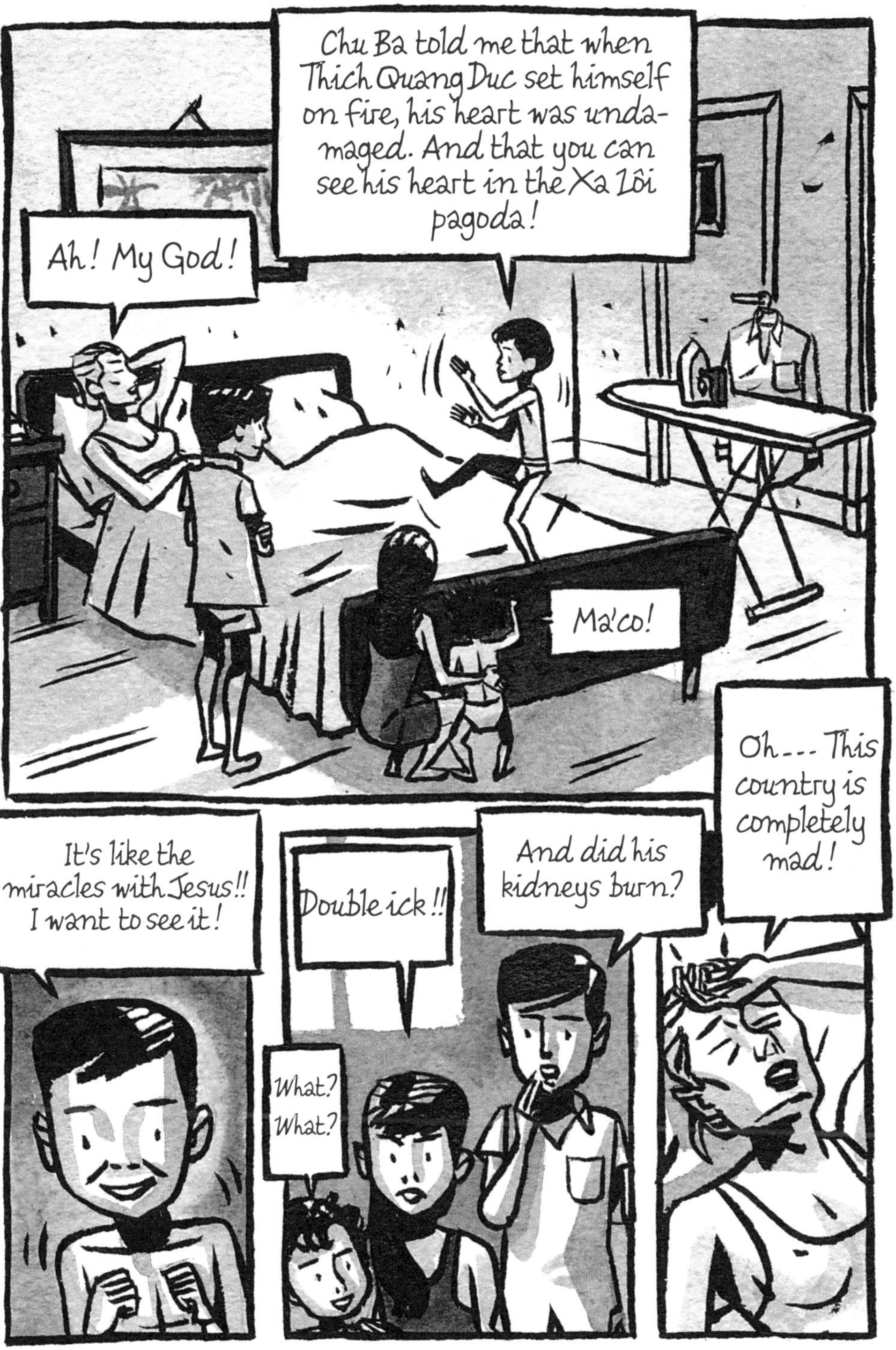
Chu Ba told me that when Thich Quang Duc set himself on fire, his heart was undamaged. And that you can see his heart in the Xa Lôi pagoda!
Ah! My God!
Ma'co!
Oh... This country is completely mad!
It's like the miracles with Jesus!! I want to see it!
Double ick!!
And did his kidneys burn?
What? What?

Around that same time, President Diêm had a private talk with Papa. At the end of the day, Diêm often worked in his monastic room in the Gia Long Palace.

A short time later, Papa was offered a position as counselor at the Vietnamese Embassy in London.

Our departure was very abrupt. I have no memory of moving, saying fare-well to our Vietnamese family, to Chi Hai and Chu Ba ---

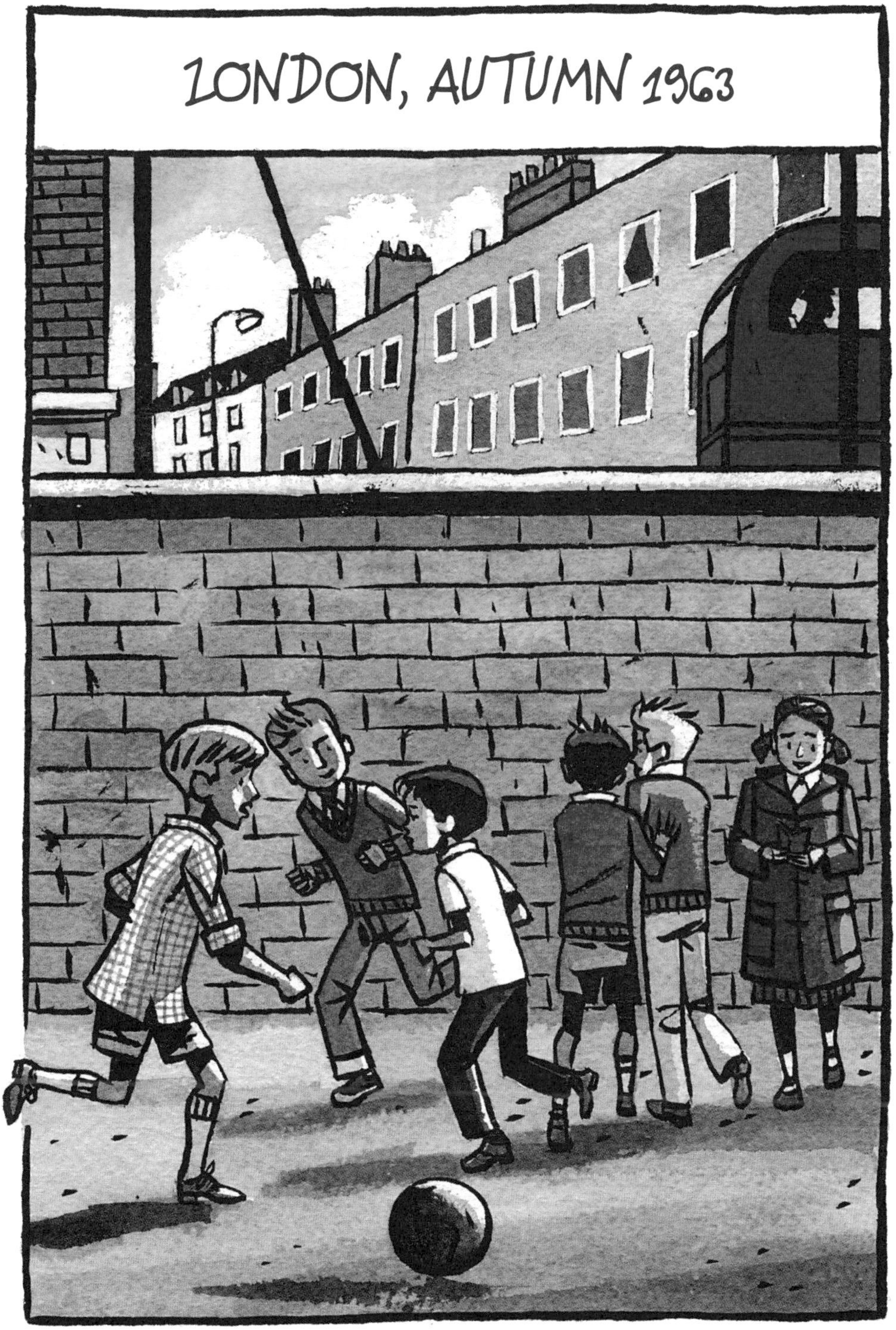
LONDON, AUTUMN 1963

My first memories of London are of the playground at the French school. I was 6 years old.

246

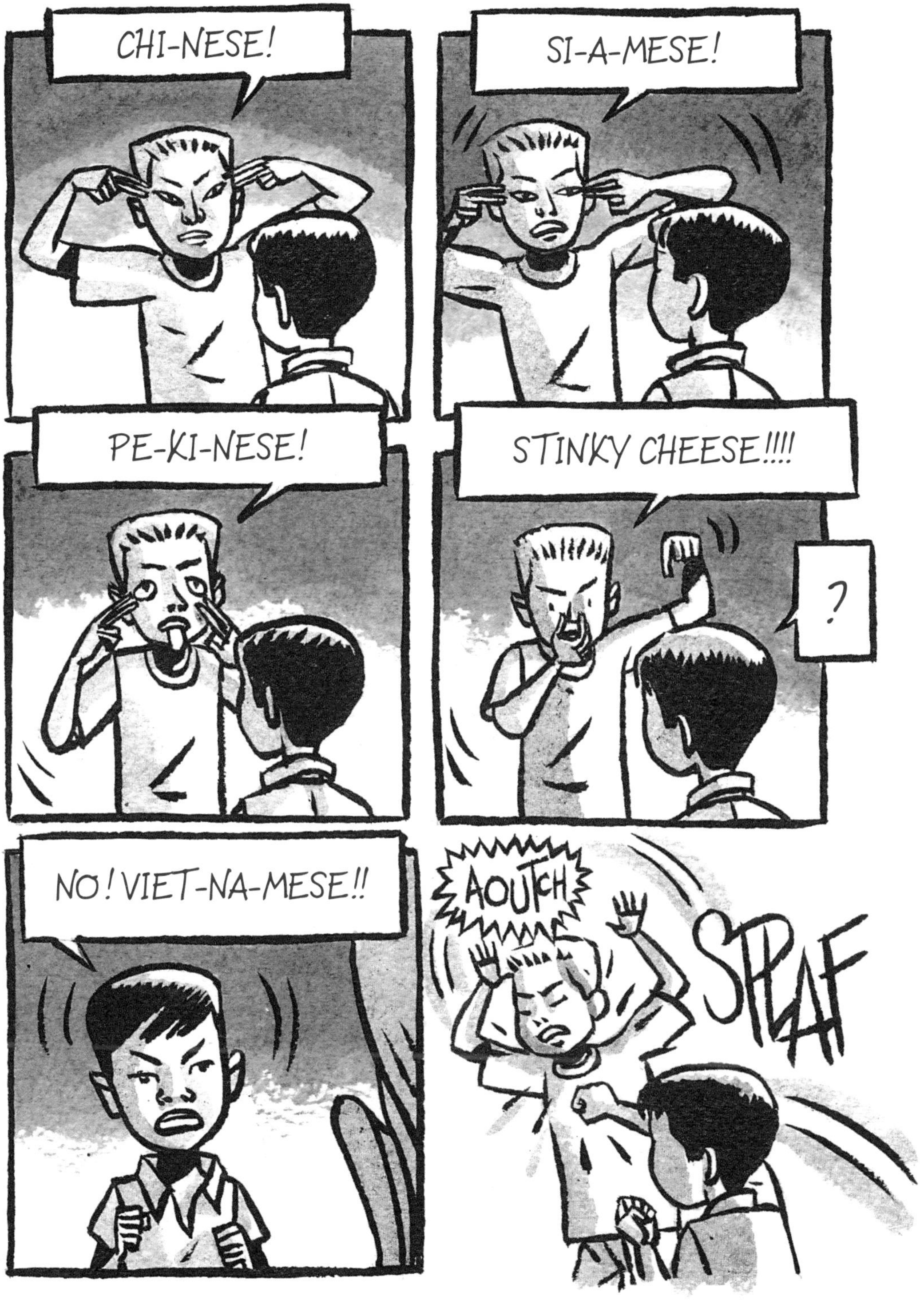
CHI-NESE!
SI-A-MESE!
PE-KI-NESE!
STINKY CHEESE!!!!
?
NO! VIET-NA-MESE!!
AOUTCH
SPLAF

Our apartment belonged to the Vietnamese embassy, and gave onto a square with a private garden for the residents.

Even Papa, who was normally of legalistic mind, was irritated by the tone of the letter of reprimand he received soon after.

* £15: the weekly salary of a London bus driver.

We followed the news from Vietnam closely.

In South Vietnam, the Buddhist crisis is entering a new phase---

Call Papa, Domi!

Papa! News! Vietnam!

Madame Nhu, Vietnam's First Lady, commented on the recent immolations by saying —quote—that these "were a barbecue held with American imported fuel---"

No! Not Vietnam again! Haven't you had enough of war stories? Come on, boys, go out and get some fresh air!

Papa! Papa!

She can't! She really wants to feed the fire!

Mama, when I grow up, I want to be a Horse Guard!

THE WEAPONS SPEAK

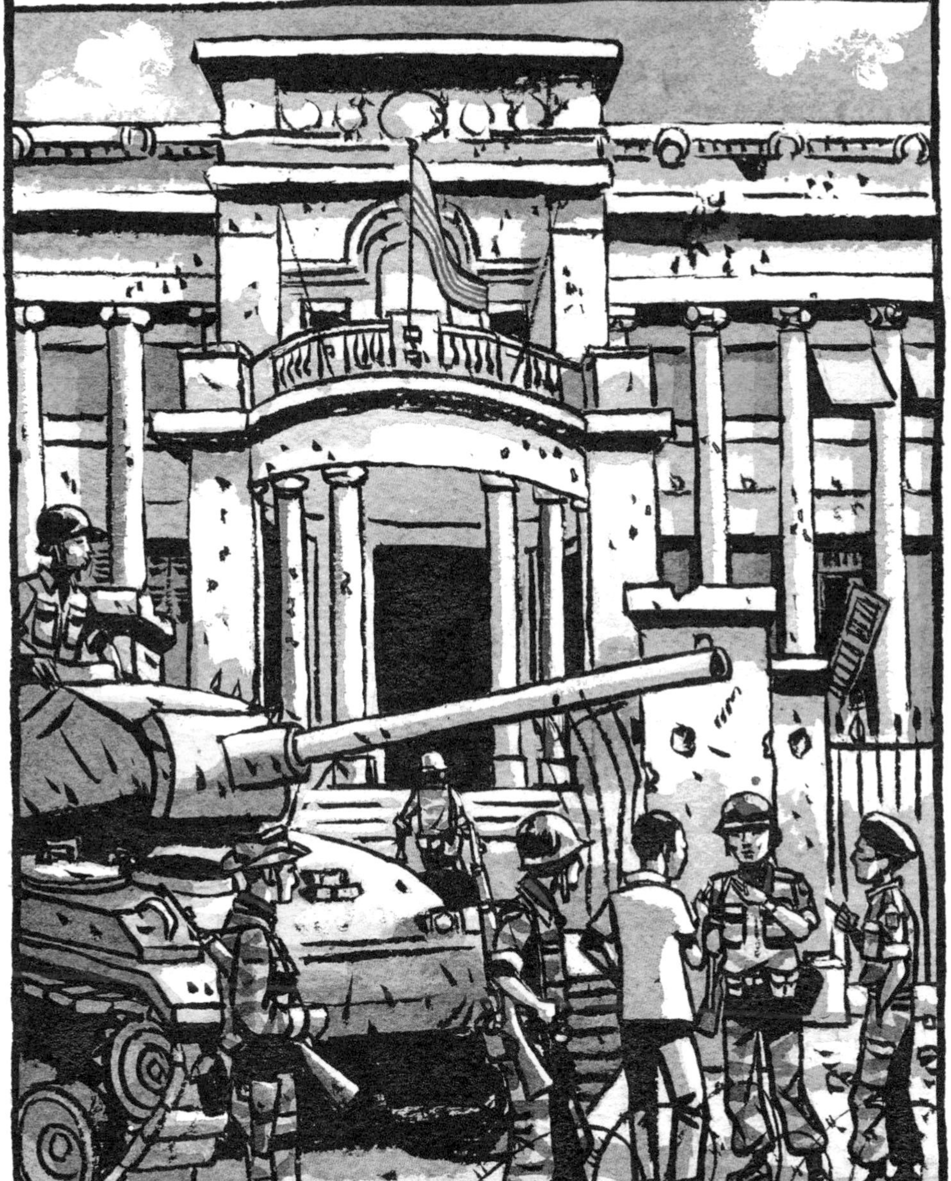

Madame Nhu's choice of words (the "barbecue"), as well as the violent repression led by Mr. Nhu against the Buddhists, irritated Kennedy, who named a new ambassador to Vietnam.

It would be judicious to distance yourself from your brother Nhu and his impetuous wife.

Our president assures you of the United States' support.

Washington will never tell me what to do!

Thank him in the name of the Vietnamese people fighting for freedom.

Henry Cabot-Lodge

Ngô Dinh Diêm

The Americans began considering the possibility of a coup d'état.

I don't support a coup, but Diêm has to be more cooperative!

John F. Kennedy

We are in contact with the Vietnamese generals who want a change in the power structure, Mr. President!

Henry Cabot-Lodge

After several false alarms, the coup d'état was launched on November 1, 1963 by South Vietnamese generals.

We have the green light from the Americans.

They'd rather stay in the shadows --- They like it that way!

Well, that's good! This is Vietnamese business.

The palace was surrounded and after a brief skirmish with the Guard, it was captured and pillaged.

Look at this! Madame Nhu's nightgown!

Diêm and Nhu have escaped!

The president and his brother had fled through a tunnel leading to a house near the palace. A car took them to Cho Lon, the Chinese section of Saigon, where they hid in the church of Saint Francis Xavier.

In the wee hours, a detachment came to arrest them.

During the trip to the conspirators' HQ, Diêm and his brother Nhu were stabbed, then finished off with a pistol. A deliberate order or a mistake? No one ever knew.

An exuberant crowd decapitated the statue of the Trung Sisters, and their stone heads were paraded through the streets of Saigon.

When news of the coup reached Madame Nhu, she was on an official visit to the United States.

* Down with Old Lady Nhu!

The following year, two postage stamps commemorating the November 1, 1963 putsch were issued. Like the Communists, the perpetrators of the coup characterized their power grab as a "revolution."* Here is the stamp showing the army breaking the chains of oppression.

The "Diêmocracy" was certainly very unpopular, and acted shamefully at times. But to call a coup d'état a revolution! Definitely, in Vietnam, all our "liberators," be they on the right or the left, prefer to speak with weapons rather than ballot boxes.

* Cách mạng: revolution.

Three weeks later, on November 22, 1963, President Kennedy himself was assassinated in Dallas; the circumstances remain unclear.

Among the many hypotheses surrounding his death, the one relating to his commitment to Vietnam is convincing. Before his assassination, Kennedy was considering a progressive pull-out of American advisors deployed there.

The American military-industrial complex, when informed of the possibility of a withdrawal, would have wanted to eliminate the troublemaker JFK. Enormous profits were at stake.

Let's get rid of that snotty-nosed double-crossing democrat!

You want to kill the president of the United States?

A plausible reason. Among others. In any case, JFK's successor, Lyndon B. Johnson of Texas, fearing accusations of being soft on Communism, sank ever deeper into the Vietnamese quagmire.

It's like the Alamo. Someone has to go and help out. And we're going to help out Vietnam, for God's sake!

In South Vietnam, the year after Diêm fell was full of instability, with riots and one coup after another.

In the midst of the disorder, the NLF guerrillas strengthened their position.

At the end of '64, a young general, Nguyên Van Thiêu, was able to take over with the help of the US. In the South as in the North, the military was in power.

I am taking the destiny of our country in hand.

Out of a sense of duty, Papa would have continued serving his country, but the future was uncertain and Mama's mental health fragile.

This merry-go-round of generals is grotesque. They have no legitimacy!

As long as you're not called back to Vietnam. I'd go mad!

In October '64, he submitted his resignation to the ambassador in London.

Thanks to the British journalists he met in Vietnam, Papa was recruited as a translator for Reuters on Fleet Street.

We will miss you!

The bombing of North Vietnam is intensifying ...

CLIC CLIC

CLIC CLIC

EPILOGUE

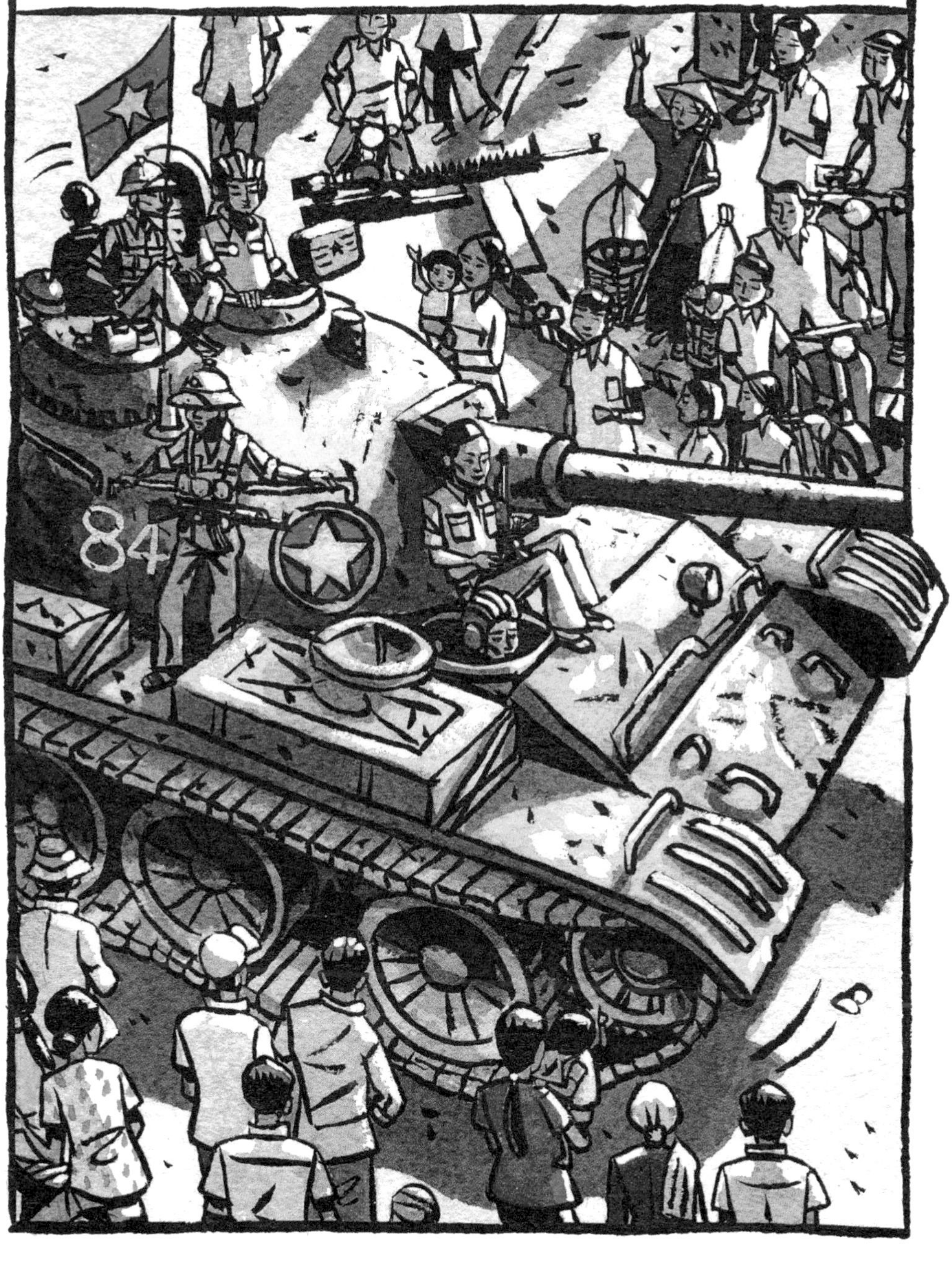
84

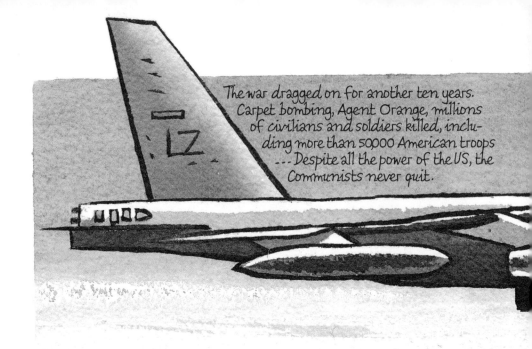

The war dragged on for another ten years. Carpet bombing, Agent Orange, millions of civilians and soldiers killed, including more than 50,000 American troops --- Despite all the power of the US, the Communists never quit.

The Vietnam War *divided* generations. People were either hawks --- or doves.

Peace!

Peace!

WOODSTOCK
OR
BUST

Very critical—often, rightly so—of American involvement, leftists in the West were also completely blind to the Stalinist and Maoist leanings of the Hanoi regime, which was strongly supported by the Communist bloc.

In 1972, President Richard Nixon—a hawk if there ever was one—normalized relations with Mao's China. This surprise diplomatic move helped him begin withdrawing US troops from Vietnam. The South Vietnamese were to take over; it was called "Vietnamization." People could go on killing each other, but now both sides would be Asian.

The war remained on the front pages for another three years, thanks to photos like the one of the little girl burned by napalm, Phan Thi Kim Phuc. Vietnamese photographer Nick Ut (real name, Huynh Cong Ut) won a Pulitzer Prize for the picture in 1972.

This photo was the last straw: international opinion declared the American war odious.

Ironically enough, the napalm was *dropped* by a Skyraider from a South Vietnamese squadron. No American was involved. Ut now lives in California.

The little girl from the photo survived, grew up in a socialist Vietnam, and married a Vietnamese in Cuba in 1992. Under cover of their honeymoon, the young couple defected during a stop-over in Canada. Kim Phuc now lives in Ontario and has two children.

In 1975, the South suddenly collapsed, overwhelmed by the Communist offensive. Saigon fell—or was liberated, depending on one's viewpoint—on April 30, 1975.

265

Our liberators weren't democratic in the Western sense of the word. A single, all-powerful party in power --- an ideological monolith --- a military that was considered sacred --- the opposition, all but silenced ---

* Triên lam: exhibition

Re-education camps for former puppets --- sealed borders --- boat people fleeing the country --- police surveillance --- privileges for a small number of apparatchiks and poverty for everyone else ---

Quyêt bao vê dât nuoc: Determined to defend the homeland !

Forty years later, Vietnam has opened up and life has become easier, but the spartan heroes of yesterday—or their *descendants*—have become red capitalists whose unspoken motto is "Get rich and forget about politics."

The Party enjoys a political monopoly. And the Party is rotten to the core. To hell with social justice, it's every man for himself! Is this what so many died for?

Our desire to live in a non-Communist country was legitimate!

Yes, but we should recognize that our methods were obscenely violent.

The Americans wanted to take things in hand, thinking they would do better than us. And with their strength...

They wanted a rich man's war. The temptation of any developed country: use technology and spare the soldiers.

We should have done it on our own, with American weapons, but without their soldiers, the way the Communists did: the USSR and China provided the material, and the PCVN* supplied the labor. The mere presence of American GIs made us lose face.

We wouldn't have lasted long, since we were less battle-hardened and disciplined than the Communists. But there would have been fewer deaths.

* The Vietnamese Communist Party

270

Don't forget that the Communist revolution promised independence, justice, and land reform. An irresistible credo sanctified by the suffering—I'd even say martyrdom – that was endured. We had nothing so romantic to offer ---

Look! There's Mother!

I see!

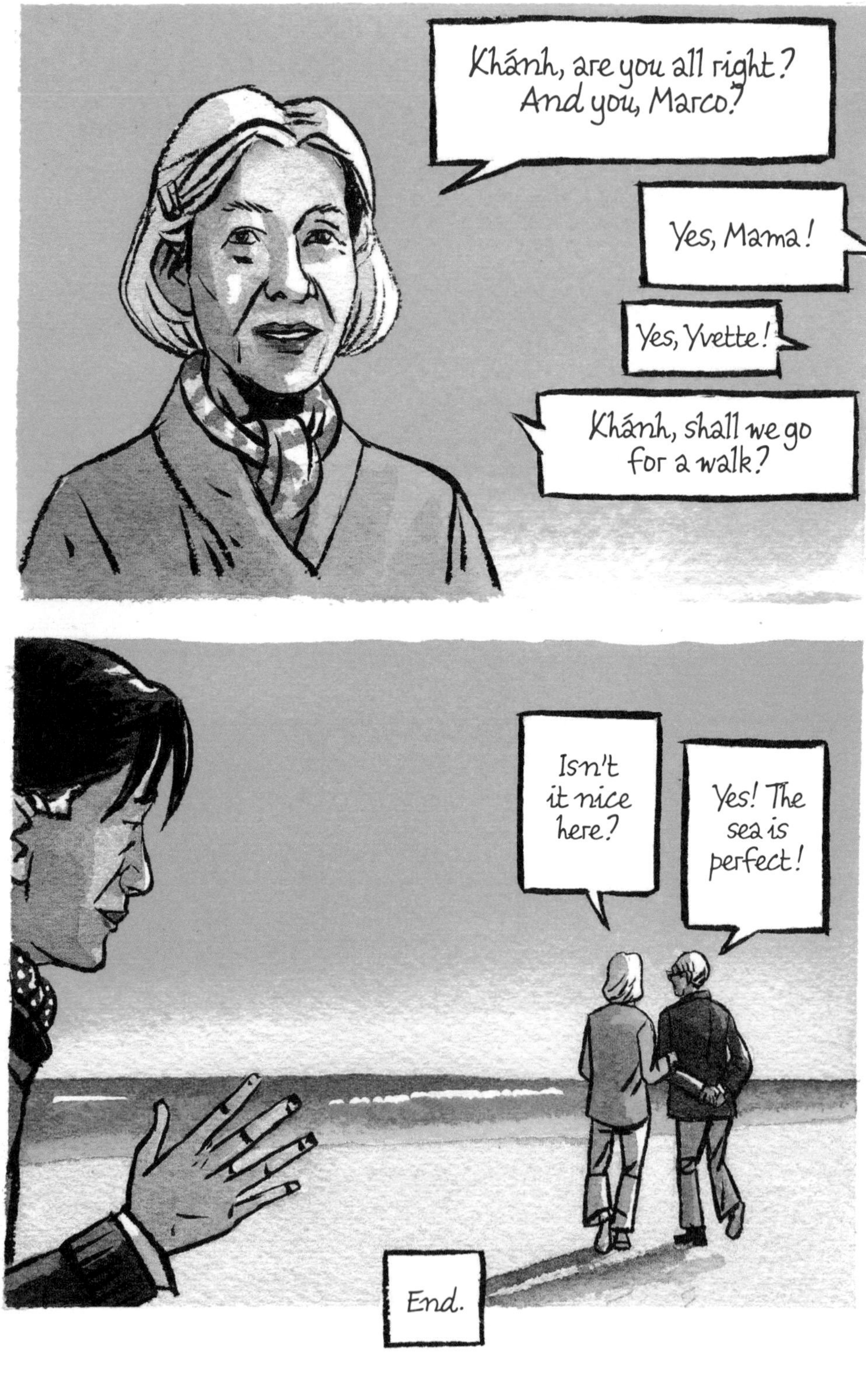
Khánh, are you all right? And you, Marco?
Yes, Mama!
Yes, Yvette!
Khánh, shall we go for a walk?
Isn't it nice here?
Yes! The sea is perfect!
End.

My father Truong Buu Khánh died in Saint-Malo on June 2, 2012, just as I was finishing the drawings for this book.

For my father Truong Buu Khánh and my mother Yvette, née Horel.
For my brother Dominique-Ai My and my sisters Mireille-Mai and Anh-Noëlle.
For my Vietnamese and French family.

My thanks to Jean-Luc Fromental, Marie-Christine Courtès, Truong Buu Diên, Truong Diêu-Lan, Mireille-Mai Truong, Anh-Noëlle Truong, Paloma, Capucine and Prune Truong, Vincent Tôn Van, Ly Chanh Trung, Vo Trung-Dung, Pierre Brocheux, Philippe Dumont, Sophie Dutertre, Jean-Yves Pham Ngoc Thuân, Paul and Jacqueline Bang-Rouhet, Pierre and Madeleine Ta-Trung, Françoise Hessel, Gérard Boivineau, Alphonse Lê Ba Muu, Dao Thanh Huyên, Ta Thi Thu-Cuc, Anne-Sophie Vo-Paillaud, Philippe and Huong Papin, Olivier and Huong Page, Marion Tigréat, and Alain Blaise.

Marcelino Truong is an illustrator, painter, and author. Born the son of a Vietnamese diplomat in 1957 in the Philippines, he and his family moved to America (where his father worked for the embassy) and then to Vietnam at the outset of the war. He attended the French Lycee in London, then moved to Paris where he earned degrees in law at the Paris Institute of Political Studies, and English literature at the Sorbonne. *Saigon Calling: London 1963-75*, a sequel to *Such a Lovely Little War*, was published by Arsenal Pulp Press in 2017.

David Homel (translator) is a writer, journalist, filmmaker, and translator. His most recent novel is *The Fledgings* (Cormorant Books). He has translated many French-language books, and is a two-time Governor General's Literary Award winner. He lives in Montreal.